# ISAIAH

**BIBLE STUDY COMMENTARY**

# ISAIAH

## BIBLE STUDY COMMENTARY

## D. DAVID GARLAND

**ZONDERVAN**
**PUBLISHING HOUSE** OF THE ZONDERVAN CORPORATION
GRAND RAPIDS, MICHIGAN 49506

Library of Congress Catalog Card Number 68-58077

ISBN 0-310-24853-1

*Printed in the United States of America*

Dedicated to Jane Ellen and
David Marshall whose lives
have been nothing but a
joy to their mother and me.

# Preface

This study guide to the book of Isaiah represents an attempt to present one approach to the book. It is not a critical study. It was written with the layman in mind and with the hope that he will read it alongside the open Bible.

To best accomplish the purpose in the writing of this study guide the student should first read the verse or section under consideration in the book of Isaiah and then consider the discussion which attempts at least one explanation of that section from the Bible.

This book is not an endeavor to write a full and exhaustive commentary on the book of Isaiah but is an attempt to furnish a guide for the study of the book.

The author is indebted to Zondervan Publishing House, Grand Rapids, Michigan, for requesting the manuscript; my teachers for my love of the prophets; and the many who have contributed to my own understanding through their speaking and writing. A special indebtedness is to be acknowledged to Mrs. Harry Hickman for having edited the final draft. Her contribution has been invaluable. A great debt is owed Miss Nancy Norman, my secretary, for her assistance in typing the initial drafts; Mrs. Charles Parker, a student at the Southwestern Baptist Theological Seminary, Fort Worth, Texas for typing most of the final draft; and Mrs. Daniel Zellner for typing the last chapter of the final draft, the preface and study questions.

D. DAVID GARLAND

*Southwestern Baptist Theological Seminary*
*Fort Worth, Texas, 76122*

# Contents

**BIBLE STUDY
COMMENTARY**

ISAIAH

CHAPTER 1

# Introducing the Prophet

## (Isaiah 1:1, 6:1)

About the time Amos was beginning his ministry to Israel and some years before Hosea appeared, Isaiah was born in Jerusalem (*ca.* 765-760 B.C.). He, like the other eighth-century prophets, lived during a time of unparalleled prosperity with all its attendant evils. And he, like the others, spent his life trying to save his nation from the consequences of these evils.

1. *The Prophet's Personal History.* Though little information is available concerning the personal life of Isaiah, it is believed that his entire ministry was spent in Judah. According to tradition, his father, Amoz (not to be confused with Amos), was a brother of Amaziah. If this is true, Isaiah and Uzziah, Judah's eleventh king, were cousins. Though concrete evidence is lacking, there seems to be some basis for this theory. In the first place, usage of "iah" in a person's name is believed to have been practiced almost exclusively among royalty. The Hebrew letters transliterated "iah" stand for Yahweh and were frequently compounded with another Hebrew word to form a name. The combination in this instance means "salvation of Yahweh." If this was a practice used exclusively or predominantly by royalty, then there seems to be some support for the tradition that Isaiah was related to the royal line and may have indeed been the cousin of Uzziah.

7

A second evidence supporting a close relationship, even kinship, between the king and Isaiah is the accessibility of the king and the court to the prophet. The accounts of his contacts with the king and the court do not suggest the usual solemnity accorded kings. But this may infer Isaiah's close relationship — only royalty would have such ready access to the king and the court (7:1-9).

Isaiah was married (8:3) and the father of at least two sons, Shear-jashub (7:3) and Maher-shalal-hash-baz (8:1-4). Shear-jashub was between seven and nine years of age when he accompanied his father at the time of Isaiah's confrontation with Ahaz around 735 B.C. His brother, Maher-shalal-hash-baz, was born a year or so after that now famous meeting with Ahaz.

The names of both sons have symbolic meaning. Shear-jashub means "a remnant shall return." Maher-shalal-hash-baz means "speed the spoil, haste the booty." "Shear-jashub" suggests that from Judah there would be a remnant which would survive God's judgment and be restored to become the nucleus of the kingdom of God. "Maher-shalal-hash-baz" implies a speedy doom for Judah's enemies, Syria and Israel, and a subsequent freedom for Judah from their oppressive threats.

Isaiah was called to his prophetic ministry in "the year that king Uzziah died," around 742 B.C. (6:1). If the prophet was born between 765-760 B.C., he would have been twenty years old at the time of his call. According to late Christian and Jewish tradition, Isaiah prophesied until the beginning of the reign of Manasseh (*ca.* 686 B.C.), when he was slain. Some historians believe that Isaiah lived ten years longer. If this latter date is correct, Isaiah had a ministry in excess of half a century and died at the age of seventy-five or eighty.

  2. *The Political and Military Conditions in Judah During the Ministry of Isaiah.* Generally, the conditions in Judah during the ministry of Isaiah were the same as those Amos and Hosea preached against in Israel. In fact, there were many parallels between the practices and conditions in the two countries. For example, during the time that Jeroboam II was expanding the territorial holding of Israel, Uzziah was attempting to do the same in Judah. Militarily Judah was strong. This made possible long hoped for victories over the Philistines and the Arabians (II Chronicles 26:6, 7). Uzziah also exacted tribute from Ammon (II Chronicles 26:8). The conquest of the southern regions of the Negeb secured trade routes in

Arabia as well as established control over the port of Elath, so vital to international trade (II Chronicles 26:2).

While the king was busy with his external expansion, he did not neglect the internal strengthening of the nation. He built fortifications at Jerusalem (II Chronicles 26:9); he reorganized the army into a strong offensive organization as well as a formidable weapon of defense (II Chronicles 26:13, 14). In addition, he accumulated a great store of war material to counter any threat to the security of Judah (II Chronicles 26:15).

Uzziah was eventually succeeded by his son Jotham (742-735 B.C.), who had served as coregent from *ca.* 750 B.C. Jotham continued the policies which had been initiated by his father and as a result reigned in relative security until he was faced with the threat posed by the Syro-Ephramitic coalition (*ca.* 735 B.C.). This was an attempt to force Judah to join with Syria and Israel (Ephraim) in a revolt against Assyria. The threat did not reach critical proportions, however, until the accession of Jotham's son Ahaz (735-715 B.C.). When forced to make a decision in face of the threat, Ahaz, rather than acceding to the counsel of Isaiah not to fear the foe (Chapter 7:1-9), petitioned Assyria for aid. Assyria responded by punishing the allies. But in having secured independence from Syria and Ephraim, Ahaz had lost it to the Assyrians. Henceforth the nation would be subservient to Assyria until that powerful nation declined and was replaced by the Babylonians.

Upon the death of Ahaz, Hezekiah ascended to the throne (715-687 B.C.). During his early reign, he remained in good stead with the Assyrians. But around 711 B.C. Israel's neighbors, those subservient to the Assyrians, plotted a revolt. This revolt was known as the Ashdod Rebellion and was initially supported by Judah, but she withdrew from the plot in time to be spared the humiliation of defeat by the Assyrian forces (Isaiah 20:1). After this Judah remained a vassal until the end of the eighth century when, under the leadership of a strong pro-Egyptian faction, she again revolted. Sennacherib, preoccupied with threatened revolt in the east, did not immediately respond to the threat; but after subduing the eastern rebels, he turned toward the west. His troops overran Tyre, Sidon, and most of Judah (II Kings 18). They finally stood outside the gates of the Holy City threatening its destruction. But Yahweh would not allow the presumption of Sennacherib. He intervened, the forces of Assyria were devastated, and the king left for home (II Kings 19:35 ff.). Jerusalem was saved.

Beyond these significant events, little is known of the last years of Hezekiah. He died between 697 and 686 B.C. — perhaps closer to 686 B.C. and was succeeded by Manasseh.

According to tradition, Isaiah was sawn asunder by order of Manasseh soon after the new monarch ascended the throne.

3. *The Economic Condition in Judah at the Time of Isaiah.* After subjugating the outlying areas and securing of the nation within, Uzziah began to expand and develop trade with the world at large — along the trade routes which ran through Arabia to the port of Elath and from there to the maritime nations of the world. This trade pushed the already healthy economy to a point comparable to the "golden age" of David and Solomon.

Along with these economic developments there were concerted efforts to make the land itself produce more. Agricultural programs were instituted and expanded. These included a more extensive cultivation of the fields and the vineyards in the country and a conscious effort to increase the number of cattle. Many new cisterns were dug to assure the supply of water required by the expanding industries (II Chronicles 26:10).

These resources furnished Ahaz with a strong base from which to bargain with Assyria for protection against the threat of Syria and Damascus. Surely the Assyrians had a price which only a prosperous nation could afford. Evidently Ahaz was willing to pay whatever was demanded. It cost the nation in more ways than one. Many feel that this decision determined the destiny of Judah for centuries.

4. *The Social, Moral, and Religious Conditions in Judah at the Time of Isaiah's Ministry.* Though the nation had made great economic, military, and political strides during this period, all was not well in Judah. She had neglected her social, moral, and religious obligations.

The materialism of the era had infested the nobles with possessions' twin — greed. Monopolies of ownership were established so the more fortunate could demand exorbitant rents from the poor. Then when they could not pay, the poor found themselves forced into slavery (Isaiah 5:8). These powerful and influential individuals were also instrumental in the perversion of justice (Isaiah 5:22, 23). In fact, the unscrupulous judges had joined them in their devious methods (Micah 3:11).

In addition to the cruelties perpetuated by greed and injustice, the times were marked by widespread drunkenness and revelry (Isaiah 5:11, 12). Taxes had been increased until they had become an excessive burden (Micah 3:10). It was a dark and foreboding picture which Isaiah saw as he studied the conditions within Judah.

Religiously, the picture was no more encouraging. Judah had been compromised through Ahaz's introduction of paganism into the nation to satisfy the ruler of Assyria (II Kings 16:10 ff.). This was in addition to those already conducted at unauthorized centers established during the reign of Solomon which were still standing as late as the era of the reforms of Josiah a hundred years later than Isaiah (II Kings 23:13). These things alone would seem to suggest that the reforms — even those of Hezekiah (II Kings 18) — may not have been as effective nor as long lasting as some have previously thought. Yet, these factors are not to be taken as evidence of a lessening in religious activity. There seems to have been much, but it was formal, and lacking in genuineness and sincerity. Though sacrifices were being made with studied regularity they were nothing more than vain oblations (Isaiah 1:13). As a result their new moons and feasts had become a burden to Yahweh (Isaiah 1:14). The reason was obvious. There was a contradiction between ritual practice and character. If they ever expected their ritual to be acceptable they would have to

> "put away the evil of your doings . . . cease to do evil; learn to do well; seek judgement, relieve the oppressed, judge the fatherless, plead for the widow" (Isaiah 1:16, 17, ASV).

In other words, Isaiah was warning them that both their conduct and character must be compatible with the ideal suggested by their religious performance. Isaiah castigated them for the conditions which he found in society (Isaiah 1:21 ff.) — conditions which betrayed the genuineness of their ritual. He declared that their sacrifices, as a result, meant nothing to Yahweh (Isaiah 1:11). They were, in fact, abominable to Him (Isaiah 1:13).

Such weaknesses placed the nation in grave peril, and this Isaiah tried to impress upon them through his counsel and preaching. Even though he did not always succeed, they always knew there had been a prophet among them.

5. *The Date and Authorship of the Book of Isaiah.* Although there is a diversity of opinion as to who wrote the sixty-six chapters of Isaiah, all scholars would insist on the prophet's historicity and his having at least a significant part in the writing of the book called

by his name. Those who reject the unity of Isaiah 1-66 usually divide the book into three major sections: 1-39; 40-55; and 56-66. The first section is often referred to as Isaiah or First Isaiah. According to many scholars the writings of the prophet are contained in these chapters. Some limit his material to 1-12 and some shorter sections in 13-39. The remainder of the material they assign to a date later than Isaiah and attribute it to an unknown author or to the School of Isaiah. The second section (40-55), usually called Deutero-Isaiah, is dated in the time of the exile and is assigned to an unknown writer dwelling among those taken to Babylon. The third section (56-66), often referred to as Trito-Isaiah, is usually assigned to one or more writers living in the period subsequent to the return from the Babylonian captivity.

There are those, on the other hand, who reject the concept of multiple authorship for the book of Isaiah. They contend that tradition has always held that the book was written by the prophet. They cite the Dead Sea Scrolls as a more recent evidence supporting the unity of the book since there are no divisions indicated in the Isaiah scroll. Therefore, it is contended, that until a satisfactory explanation of the tradition is given, the authorship by the prophet is defensible.

## FOR FURTHER STUDY OR DISCUSSION

1. What international factors allowed and contributed to the conditions prevailing in Judah during Isaiah's ministry?

2. Who were the other canonical prophets whose ministries were during the same general period as Isaiah? How did they differ in approach from Isaiah?

3. Read the account of Uzziah's reign in II Kings 15, II Chronicles 26. Then read the article on "Uzziah" in *The Interpreter's Dictionary of the Bible,* Volume IV, pp. 742-744 or *The Zondervan Pictorial Bible Dictionary,* p. 879.
   (From this point on *The Interpreter's Dictionary of the Bible* will be referred to as IDB and *The Zondervan Pictorial Bible Dictionary* as ZPBD.)

4. List the conditions in Israel which paralleled those in Judah.

5. Read the account of the rise and establishment of the Assyrian

Empire under the leadership of "Tiglath-Pileser III" in IDB, Volume IV, pp. 641, 642 and ZPBD, p. 853.

6. What effect, if any, did the fall of Samaria have on Judah?

7. What parallels may be found between conditions in Isaiah's day and our own? What do these parallels seem to suggest? Do these parallels add significance to the message of the prophet?

8. Did religious activity mean Judah was really religious in Isaiah's day? If so, how? If not, why not? Is there a significance here for us in our own day?

CHAPTER 2

# The Agonies of an Ideal

(Isaiah 1:2—6:13)

Isaiah was an idealist. No other Old Testament prophet reached the idealistic heights which he attained. Yet there was a remarkable realism in what he said and did; his ministry was based upon maintaining a constructive tension between the actual and the ideal. At one time his message began with the ideal and worked back to the actual; at another time he began with the actual and worked up to the ideal. In either approach the primary consideration reflected his reaction to the human response to the favor and/or will of God. Isaiah began his book by recounting, very realistically, the response of Judah to Yahweh's favor and purpose.

1. *The Unreasonableness of Sin* (1:2-31). After a short superscription, which identifies the author and the period in which he lived (1:1), the prophet delivers Yahweh's indictment of Judah and Jerusalem.

(a) THE TRAGEDY OF REBELLIOUS CHILDREN (1:2-3). No nation in human history had experienced so many acts of Yahweh's kindness as had Israel. Yahweh had found the nation in bondage, had delivered her from the Egyptians, had made a covenant with her, and had given her a land flowing with milk and honey (cf. Amos 2:9-12; Hosea 8:12; 9:10; 11:3). Through these acts of kindness God had made great and exalted a nation in which He set His hopes. But, despite all His benefits, and without the least expression of gratitude, both Israel and Judah had rebelled against Yahweh (1:2, 4). Heaven and earth were called to witness Yahweh's indictment (1:2).

14

Judah's rebellion was not just the rebellion of a nation against a god. It was a rebellion of children against a father (1:2). Their reaction was most unreasonable. In fact, Isaiah said that the ox and donkey, who lacked the capacity to reason, demonstrated a greater sense of acknowledgment (appreciation) and dependence upon a master than did "his children," Judah upon their God (1:3). In other words, had Judah stopped to consider her origin and Yahweh's providence, she would have been forced to a sense of acknowledgment and dependence like that expressed by the animals at least. But she did not. By her actions she denied Yahweh.

(b) THE RESULTS OF DENYING YAHWEH (1:4-9). Judah's denials of Yahweh had led the people into "sin," (to err from the path of right and duty), "iniquity" (to be crooked or to pervert), "evil doing" (to be morally wicked, especially in relationships with others) and "corrupt dealings" (to practice deeds which result in destruction comparable to that of an invading army) (1:4). These reactions revealed that the nation had not just neutrally ignored Yahweh, but she had positively "forsaken Jehovah" for her own wicked practices. In doing so, the people had "spurned" Yahweh. In choosing their sinful ways, they had spurned their one hope of moving to God. Their rebellion resulted in retrogression. "They are turned away backward" (1:4c). Rather than moving toward Yahweh's ideal, they were moving away from it at an unbelievable risk.

No people, chosen (redeemed) or otherwise, can flaunt themselves in the face of the gracious God of Israel with impunity. The very choice of sin over the will of God must inevitably result in retribution. Judah had already suffered greatly at the hand of the One whom she had spurned. The nation was marked by sickness. There was no soundness to be found in her (1:5b, 6a). "Wounds," "bruises," and "fresh stripes" are the figures Isaiah used to depict her tragic affliction. As a man had been beaten and bruised by a just master, so had Judah been beaten. Her wounds and bruises had not been bound up nor treated. She had been left in her desperate strait. Not one remedy had been applied to the languishing population (1:6b).

The country had been brought to these tragic conditions by Yahweh's sending enemies against her because of rebellion and sin (1:7). The "strangers" may refer to the Syrians, Philistines (II Chronicles 28:18), or, as some suggest, may look ahead to the

Assyrians in 701 B.C. Because of the nation's rejection of Yahweh, Jerusalem was left as insecure as a frail watchman's hut perched on four poles in the midst of a cultivated area (1:8). (These huts were not strong and were liable to be overturned with very little effort.) Jerusalem was in grave peril. She was "as a besieged city." Had it not been for a gracious act on Yahweh's part the city would "have been as Sodom" and "Gomorrah" (1:9). This is evidently a reference to the Sennacherib crisis in which Jerusalem was spared by a miraculous deliverance (II Kings 19:35 ff.)

(c) JUDAH'S ATTEMPT TO PURCHASE YAHWEH'S FAVOR (1:10-17). In verses 10-12, the prophet described the ineffectual response of the nation to Yahweh's extraordinary deliverance. It manifested their basic attitude toward Yahweh. The people believed that they could, through their heartless ritualistic practices, purchase Yahweh's favor, and yet refuse to give attention to His laws and teachings (1:10). Such a variance between form and practice could not go unchallenged. Yahweh, therefore, revealed through Isaiah that He had had enough "of the burnt-offerings of rams, and the fat of fed beasts; . . . the blood of bullocks, or of lambs, or of he goats" (1:11). Sacrifices alone would never suffice. This kind of religious activism had never been required by their God (1:12) and would not now be acceptable. What He required was a quality of life commensurate with the highest and noblest type of ritual activity — an activity which reflects the true attitude of the heart and life — not a false attempt to buy His favor.

In light of the nation's attempt to deceive Him by ritual, Yahweh directed the people to cease bringing "vain," that is, meaningless, empty, sacrifices to be offered up to Him. It was positively abominable and iniquitous to Him (1:13). Their "new moons and . . . appointed feasts" had become objects of contempt and sources of burden to Yahweh (1:14). All this had come about because the sacrifices they brought had been borne in hands full of the "blood" of murder and oppression (1:15). Yahweh would not accept sacrifices offered by hands which had been involved in oppression, injustice, and even murder (1:21).

The only way Judah could expect to have Yahweh look with favor upon her sacrifices was through an elimination of evil practices and the inauguration of works of righteousness, compassion and justice (1:16, 17). In that day Yahweh would accept the people and their sacrifices, and their cities and nation would be secure.

(d) JUDAH CALLED TO CHOOSE BETWEEN THE ALTERNATIVES (1:18-20). In verses 18-20, Yahweh entered a call for Judah to plead her cases. He stated that their "sins . . . as scarlet" and "red like crimson" would be pardoned if the alternative conditions of verses 19 and 20 were realized and the proper choices made.

Though an alternative had been offered before (1:18), they had evidently refused to respond. There followed a second (1:19, 20). It, too, was rejected.

(e) THE TRAGEDY OF CHOOSING THE WRONG ALTERNATIVE (1:21-31). With the conditions of pardon rejected, the prophet characterized Jerusalem as a city of unfaithfulness, murder, and idolatry (1:21). All that had been of value — silver and wine may be a reference to their nobles or leaders — had become as valueless as dross and watered-down wine (1:22). Their leaders had joined hands with thieves and had become involved in bribery and unjust rewards (1:23).

In light of the people's rejection of the proffered forgiveness of Yahweh and their persistence in evil, Yahweh declared that He would deal with the nation as He treated his adversaries (1:24); but by that treatment purge away the dross and alloy which had entered their lives (1:25). There would remain a purified remnant. These would turn to Yahweh and make up the population of a "city of righteousness, the faithful town" (1:26, 27). On the other hand, those who persisted in their evil way would be as tow (the refuse).

2. *The Contrast Between the Ideal and the Real* (2:1—4:6). In these three chapters are contained several oracles of Isaiah which reflect a distinct contrast between the ideal to be hoped for and promised by Yahweh and the actual conditions prevailing in Judah at the time.

(a) ZION TO BE THE SPIRITUAL CENTER OF THE UNIVERSE (2:1-5). In the latter days, the final age of world history, Yahweh planned to establish His government and thereby His authority in "the mountain of Jehovah's house" (2:2). On the basis of verse 3 it is obvious that the reference is "to the mountain of the Lord, to the house of the God of Jacob" or the Temple mount. The Temple mount is to be exalted above every other mountain and hill in the world, referring to the superior political, ethical, moral, and religious ideals to be found in the society governed by Yahweh. As a result of the quality of the instruction being given at Jerusalem, people from every

nation in the world are going to make their way to the mountain
(2:3). Yahweh had chosen this as the place in history where He
would make known His purposes for all men. Men and nations
involved in conflicts and disagreements will find Him to be an ideal
arbiter. As a result of His instructions they will be encouraged to
walk in His paths, that is, His revealed will and purpose (2:3).
When they learn His teachings and walk in His paths, then all nations will turn their instruments of war into instruments of peace,
agricultural implements, and they will not learn — neither study,
plan nor participate in — war any more (2:4). Then, in what may
have been a verse of transition, the house of Jacob was admonished
to respond to the privileges afforded in the light — revealed will and
purpose — of Yahweh (2:5).

(b) FOR REFUSING TO WALK IN THE LIGHT (2:6—4:1). Instead of following Yahweh, the people chose to fill their lives and
cities with foreign customs and practices (2:6). Also by striking
hands (forming alliances) with foreigners, they were showing a lack
of confidence in Yahweh. Possession of silver and gold became an
end in itself and they placed their hope for security upon the number
of their horses and chariots (2:7). Instead of worshiping Yahweh,
the God of creation, they bowed down to idols which they themselves
had hewn from stone or carved from wood (2:8). As a result of
these practices and attitudes the nation was soon going to be hum-
bled and brought low (2:9-10), but through His righteous judgment
Yahweh was going to be exalted (2:11).

On "the day of the Lord," judgment will fall upon their leaders
(2:19-22) and upon their possessions (2:12-18). All that they
treasure will be destroyed. Their forests, fortifications, ships, idols,
and leaders will be dealt a devastating blow.

After having outlined the judgment coming upon their possessions and leaders, the prophet described the era of anarchy to come
out of these circumstances. There will be neither food nor water
(3:1). Their leaders will be lost in the upheaval (3:2, 3) and be
replaced by fledgling princes (3:4). Society itself will be in chaos,
running from one potential leader to another in search of a stabilizing
force (3:6-8), reaping the harvest of years of leadership which had
mislead them (3:9-12).

Because of these conditions, so long tolerated and even encouraged, Yahweh will bring the nation to judgment (3:13-15). The
leaders who have kept the vineyard will be charged with having

plundered the resources of the poor rather than having secured them. They have crushed and ground out of the poor everything they had.

The last group to be doomed will be the proud arrogant women of Jerusalem (3:16—4:1). These women, who had doubtless been the principal ones to profit from the oppressive activities of the nation's leaders, are going to be denied their luxuries and finery. Instead of the finest in apparel and jewelry (3:18-23), they will wear the ropes of exile and the sackcloth of affliction. Their hair will be cut off in shame and they will be branded as cattle by their new owner (3:24). They will be denied the joys of marriage because of the devastating depletion of the male population through war (3:25—4:1). Thus will Yahweh bring down judgment upon the wicked inhabitants of Jerusalem.

(c) JERUSALEM'S FUTURE GLORY (4:2-6). After the judgment, which not only will destroy the wicked but also cleanse the survivors, a remnant will remain which will produce a branch, the Messiah. He is going to inaugurate an ideal reign and establish a just society (4:2-6). That branch, "the branch of the Lord," will be of such beauty that the remnant will glory in Him — they are the true fruit of the nation (4:2). What a contrast the Messiah will be with the present population of the nation! At last, when "the branch" comes forth and is recognized, His subjects will be recognized as holy because the city of Jerusalem will be purged of her evil, and her inhabitants will be the people of Yahweh (4:3, 4). At that time Yahweh will return to guide and protect His people from anything which would injure them (4:5, 6).

3. *The Tragedy of the Vineyard* (5:1-30). On the basis of verse 1, this chapter has been frequently called "The Song of the Vineyard." It has been suggested that the song was one which was sung in connection with one of the yearly festivals, and that Isaiah incorporated it into his prophecy to depict the relationship between Yahweh and the chosen nation. On the other hand, there are those who suggest that the prophet used one of the festivals as the occasion for the initial use of the song. In either case, the lesson is the same — the nation had failed to measure up to God's purpose for her.

(a) THE SONG OF THE VINEYARD (5:1-7). The prophet began his song by stating that it was "of my well-beloved" — Yahweh — who had given extreme care to His vineyard that it might produce the choicest fruit. He had chosen a fertile plot, had removed every impediment to growth and had planted a vine with the greatest potential (5:1, 2a). He built a tower that a guard might keep the animals and intruders away (5:2b). In happy anticipation He dug a winevat and waited for the time of harvest (5:2c). When at long last the time came to harvest the crop, there was nothing but rotten fruit (5:2d). The vine had failed in spite of all the advantages, care, and attention given it.

Therefore, the husbandman, greatly disappointed, called upon His hearers to decide whose fault it was. He asked that they indicate where He had failed in His choice and care of the vine and vineyard. The very form of the question suggests the answer: there was nothing left undone. The vine should have produced good fruit. Yet it did not; and because of that, it now will be laid waste and destroyed (5:5, 6). Then, with the lesson of the vineyard burning in their minds, the people heard this shocking news. The house of Israel was the vineyard and the men of Judah were the plant of His delight (5:7). These who had been so carefully selected and cared for that Yahweh had every right to expect good fruit — justice and righteousness — had produced a crop of violence and outcries (5:7b). In light of conditions in the nation, it could expect the same kind of treatment the vineyard had received. The day of reckoning was fast approaching and the announcement of the judgment took the form of woes.

(b) WOES UPON THE WICKED (5:8-24). A woe is the announcement of that which the wicked deserve and are to expect. The first woe was pronounced upon the powerful landholders who sought to monopolize ownership (5:8). When Yahweh comes to deal with them in judgment their houses will become a desolation (5:9) and their acreage will be denied its productivity (5:10).

The second woe was pronounced upon the intemperate and frivolous citizens (5:11, 12). They will either go into captivity (5:13) or lose their lives and be swallowed up in Sheol (the abode of the dead) (5:14).

The third woe was upon those who labored at iniquity, that is, they made evil the work of their lives (5:18). These skeptics mocked the one announcing judgment by declaring that they would believe the evil that would come upon them when they saw it (5:19).

The fourth woe was pronounced on those who "call evil good, and good evil" by word or action and who "put darkness for light, and light for darkness; that put bitter for sweet, and sweet for bitter" (5:20). They presumed to know everything themselves and rejected the counsel of the truly wise man, the prophet (5:21).

The final woe was for those who indulged themselves in drinking and who rejected the claims of those who come to them with righteous causes (5:22, 23). These will be consumed as dry grass is consumed by a raging fire and their roots will be consumed by decay and rotting (5:24).

In 5:26-30, Isaiah personalizes the judgment in the form of a powerful nation who will come upon them to destroy both the land and the people. It will be a nation with a capacity to advance rapidly (5:26), and with a remarkable alertness (5:27). The marksmanship of the destroyers will be unerring (5:28) and their grasp will be as destructive as the clutches of a lion (5:29). There will be nothing but darkness and distress as they march through Yahweh's vineyard to bring upon it what it deserves (5:30).

4. *The Inaugural Vision and Call of Isaiah* (6:1-13). The usual position of the inaugural vision and/or call of a prophet, when one is recorded, is at the first of the book bearing his name (cf. Jeremiah 1; Ezekiel 1, 2; and Jonah 1). In the case of Isaiah, however, the vision and call occur in Chapter 6. Attempts to explain the position of this material are varied. Some have held that the prophecies of Isaiah were gathered in short collections and placed in chronological order in larger sections to form the book. Since Chapter 6 is a part of one of those larger sections it may have been placed first in that section of the book consisting of the material from 6:1—9:6, or in a larger collection consisting of Chapters 6-12. Others say that it may have been placed at the end of a collection made up of Chapters 1-6. Since certain knowledge is lacking and information about the composition of Isaiah is meager, another approach to the matter of the location of Chapter 6 has been suggested. This theory posits that, after having revealed the nature and character of his ministry in Chapters 1-5, the prophet felt the need of an authenticating word so he shared his vision and call for the purpose of undergirding what he had already said and for the purpose of giving added authority to his future oracles. However one may attempt to explain the position of the vision and call of Isaiah, the location does not reflect upon the integrity of the prophet's experience.

The inaugural vision of Isaiah occurred "the year king Uzziah died" (*ca.* 742 B.C.). Whether he received his vision before or after the king's death we are not told. Isaiah may have seen Yahweh at the Temple or some other place. The place is not important; the vision is. The prophet "saw" Yahweh in the heavenly Temple seated upon a throne in royal regalia, being attended by his heavenly court (6:1). The court consisted of the seraphim (burning ones) who are spiritual beings with faces, hands, and feet, and who are described as being "above Him." Their position is not to be considered as a superior one — in order to discourage such an implication, perhaps a better translation is "around Him" or "attending Him."

The seraphim, not to be confused with the cherubim, had six wings. With two wings they covered their faces that they might not look upon the Holy God, with two wings they covered their feet that He might not look upon them (a sign of unworthiness), and with two wings they moved to carry out the instructions of the One seated upon the throne (6:2).

While Yahweh sat in majesty, authority, and glory, the seraphim cried to one another that He was holy (6:3). The term "holy" suggests the nature and character of Yahweh as contrasted with that of man. Yahweh was called the thrice Holy God. This was for emphasis. (Repetition of a term, phrase, or clause in Hebrew is the superlative.)

It was, then, the thrice Holy God who was manifesting Himself to the prophet. He was the One whose glory filled the earth. His glory is the revelation of His attributes which are manifest in Himself and His creation (6:3b).

As the seraphim spoke, the very thresholds of the heavenly Temple shook and the house was filled with smoke (6:4). This was the result of the presence of Yahweh.

It seems, however, that the most significant result of the vision was the effect it had upon Isaiah. He had "seen the King, Jehovah of hosts" (6:5c). The titles were those given the ruler of the covenant people and the creator of all the universe. To see the Holy One who created and ruled the universe impressed upon the prophet the great gulf between the prophet and Yahweh and directed him toward repentance. And Isaiah did declare himself to be "a man of unclean lips" who, because of his condition, could not honor Yahweh as the seraphim had. Having become aware of his own undone condition he declared himself to be a citizen of a nation of unclean lips (6:5b). Not only was he guilty but the whole nation was guilty. While Isaiah was in the process of declaring his own unworthiness and that of the nation, one of the seraphim flew to him with "a live coal in his hand, which he had taken with tongs from off the altar"; and touched his mouth with it . . . (6:6b, 7). In doing so, the seraphim was symbolically conveying the atoning efficacy of the altar to the lips of the prophet, and the effect was that his iniquity was taken away and his sin expiated (6:7b). The prophet was cleansed. Now he could declare Him holy, but this was not all that was involved — with man, when forgiveness is known, responsibility follows. Isaiah, after realizing his own need and having experienced forgiveness, was impressed with the needs of "a people of unclean lips." So when God asked, "Whom shall I send, and who will go for us?," the prophet immediately volunteered (6:8).

The task assigned the prophet was a hard one (6:9, 10). His ministry was to be one that would render the nation more insensitive to the will and purpose of God than it already was. Those to whom he would go were going to reject his message, their hearts growing more callous, their ears more dull, and their eyes more blind (6:10). Isaiah was commanded to declare the will and purpose of Yahweh, though men would resist so long that response would become impossible for them.

Isaiah responded with the question, "Lord, how long?" It was a query which revealed not only a concern for his own ministry but which also reflected a love and concern for those to whom he was to go. In response to Isaiah's question, Yahweh instructed him to continue until:

> "the cities be waste without inhabitant, and houses without man, and the land become utterly waste, and the Lord have removed men far away and the forsaken places be many in the midst of the land. And if there be yet a tenth in it, it also shall in turn be eaten up as a terebinth and as an oak whose stock remaineth, when they are felled; so the holy seed is the stock thereof" (6:11-13).

The mission of the prophet was to persist until the land was overrun and the people exiled. The exile, however, was not to be the end of Yahweh's purpose for the nation. Following the destruction associated with the exile, Isaiah prophesied, a tenth will survive but not for long. It will be cut down as one cuts down an oak tree and leaves the stump standing. Yet, there will still be life in the small group who survived the second destruction just as life is left in the stump. The life remaining is the holy seed and the holy seed is the remnant (6:13). Through the remnant Yahweh will continue His purpose. There will be a future. Those who survive the exile are the basis and hope of that future.

### FOR FURTHER STUDY OR DISCUSSION

1. What privileges did Israel and Judah enjoy? List several. Is there a nation in the world today with corresponding privileges? If so, which one? If so, is it living up to its responsibilities? If yes, in what ways? If not, why not?

2. Does Jehovah chastise nations to turn them from their erring ways? List those you believe to have been so chastened. On what grounds do you believe them to have been so chastened? How do you explain that some evil nations have not been chastened?

3. Do nations and individuals still seek to buy God's favor? If so, list some of the ways employed. Is it possible to use legitimate means of expressing gratitude in the wrong way? What are some of these? How may they be wrongly used?

4. In a real world is it possible to eliminate war? If so, how? Why have nations not done so? If not, why not? Is Isaiah 2:2-4 an unattainable ideal? If not, how can it or when will it be attained?

5. Read article on "Vine, Vineyards" in IDB, Volume IV, pp. 784-786.

6. What effect did the death of Uzziah have upon Judah and consequently upon Isaiah? Was he a revered ruler? Why?

7. Read discussion on "Cherubim and Seraphim" in IDB, Volume I, pp. 131, 132 and ZPBD, pp. 153 and 772. Compare the seraphim and cherubim.

# CHAPTER 3

# The Difference a Choice Makes

(Isaiah 7-12)

In the period ranging from 735 to 732 B.C., Judah found herself threatened by a coalition consisting of Syria and Israel (II Kings 15:37). The crisis had been precipitated by an attempt by Syria and Israel to force Judah to join them in a revolt against Assyria. Ahaz refused to join with the coalition and turned to Assyria for help. He did so against the counsel of Isaiah and thereby made a decision which possibly determined Judah's history for centuries to come.

1. *The Nation Threatened* (7:1-9). Ahaz was reluctant to join in the coalition between Syria and Israel, as we have noted, and was threatened with a march on Jerusalem (Isaiah 7:1, II Kings 16:5). The threat so frightened the king and his subjects that they were shaking "as the trees of the forest tremble with the wind" (7:2).

In face of the threat, Ahaz went on an inspection trip through the city. His purpose was to evaluate the strength of Jerusalem's defenses. He was "at the end of the conduit of the upper pool, in the highway of the fuller's field" checking the security of the water supply when Isaiah under divine direction, along with his son Shear-jashub, appeared before the king. He had come to encourage Ahaz to be unafraid in face of the threat of the anti-Assyrian coalition (7:3, 4). Isaiah said, "Take heed and be quiet; fear not, neither let thy heart be faint, because of these two tails of smoking firebrands"

(7:4). The coalition posed no more threat than a torch giving forth its last flickers promised light (7:4b). That which they proposed, a campaign against Judah and the setting up of a successor to Ahaz, would "not stand, neither . . . come to pass" (7:6, 7). These words were to assure Ahaz that he had nothing to fear because when the threat was over, "the head of Syria" would still be Damascus and the "head of Damascus" would still be Rezin and "the head of Ephraim" would still be Samaria with the son of Remaliah her king (7:8, 9). Neither Syria nor Israel will have added any of Judah's territory to their own. They will be, when the threat was over, what they had been at its beginning. Their attempt against Judah will have profited them nothing. In fact, the prophet revealed that "within three score and five years shall Ephraim be broken in pieces, so that it shall not be a people . . ." (7:8b). The point of reference is difficult to determine. It has been suggested that it is an indefinite reference to the time when Israel would be overthrown. In that case the reference is to her final overthrow in 722 B.C. (2 Kings 17).

In the latter part of 7:9, as a kind of summary statement, the king was told that if he did not "believe" this prophecy then he would not remain upon his throne and his nation would be overrun. Isaiah was saying, "There is no future for you or your kingdom unless you confidently trust in Yahweh to deliver you and protect you."

2. *A Sign Given* (7:10-16). After telling him that the opponents of Judah will soon burn themselves out, and that the nation will be secure if it looks to Yahweh, Isaiah offered Ahaz an opportunity to demonstrate his faith. He could ask for a sign which would not only prove the faithfulness of God, but which would also validate the words of the prophet (7:10, 11).

A sign is some extraordinary manifestation which is interpreted as a pledge of the certitude of something not yet established. It is a present guarantee of an event yet to come to pass. This sign was to be without limit as to area or extent. The whole universe was opened up as a possibility for the unusual occurence (7:11b).

The response of Ahaz is disappointing. He declares that he "will not ask, neither will [he] tempt Jehovah" (7:12). He is simply saying that he will "not put Jehovah to proof." In his refusal to ask for a sign, he was revealing his unwillingness to believe (7:9b). Rather than trusting God to keep the nation secure in the face of the Syro-Ephraimitic threat, he was declaring himself committed to Assyria, not God, as his hope of deliverance. He stated that he would not tempt Yahweh, that he would not put Him to the task of proving Himself (7:12). As a response the prophet said that it was one thing, and bad enough at that, to try the patience of men (himself), but it was of far greater consequence to try the patience of God by turning upon the offer of the sign which had been made (7:13). It has been suggested that this decision of Ahaz to reject the offer of a sign, and choose instead to depend upon Assyria, decided the fate of Jerusalem for the next two thousand years. What a difference a choice makes!

Though Ahaz had rejected the offer of a sign, Yahweh was not to be outdone. He gave Ahaz a sign in spite of his refusal and unbelief. Isaiah stated: "Therefore the Lord himself will give you a sign: behold, a virgin shall conceive, and bear a son and shall call his name Immanuel" (7:14).

Many of those who understand this passage according to the traditional messianic interpretation, as well as those who do not, agree that there are at least two aspects which deserve attention. First, the immediate context seems to suggest a concern on Yahweh's part over the threat to Judah and Jerusalem by the Syro-Ephraimitic coalition. Therefore Yahweh promised that He would be with them, a promise which was to be realized at the birth of Immanuel (God with us). The messianic interpretation of this passage identifies Immanuel as the Messiah. Those who resist this interpretation contend that a prophecy of the birth of the Messiah more than seven centuries after the time of Ahaz would have meant little, if anything, to the king. Yet, it may be that Isaiah believed that the Messiah would appear in the era just beyond the one in which he was living. After Yahweh had purged the nation, removing everything which would keep her from accomplishing His purpose, the Messianic Age would appear. On this basis it may be argued that the passage could have meant, and in fact did mean, a great deal to the prophet.

The second aspect of the passage has to do with its broader context — which seems to relate to the expectancy of the eighth century, especially Isaiah and Micah's — that an heir of the line of David would appear upon the throne and lead the nation to unparalleled glory. According to the traditional messianic interpretation, Isaiah 7:14 was a reference to the birth of that heir. This heir would be born of a young woman of virtue who had never been married. According to this view there is no problem created by translating the term often rendered "virgin" as "young woman," because both terms appear to have been used for one and the same person. In the Revised Standard Version, in Genesis 24:16 Rebekah is called "a virgin," while in Genesis 24:43 she is called "a young woman." Surely no one would suggest that she had become less virtuous between these two verses. It is contended, therefore, that one does not imply a lack of virtue when he translates the Hebrew term as "young woman" instead of "virgin." Some, in fact, suggest that the prophet purposely chose "young woman" because it was a term never used of a married person; and according to the law, every young woman would be understood to be a virgin until it had been established that she was not. In cases in which a girl was proven to be immoral, the community then carried out the judgment of the law (Deuteronomy 22:13-21).

Following up the idea that Immanuel was the person of the sign, many believe that Isaiah had received, for the first time, a picture of the personal Messiah; that from this point on, the emphasis would be upon "Immanuel" and not upon the nature and/or character of the one giving birth. He will live in a land of plenty and will eat "butter and honey," the figures for the best food available (7:15). Before the child reaches the age of two or three, the threat to Jerusalem posed by Syria and Ephraim will cease (7: 16). But with that, Judah's problems will not be over. She will then be faced with a graver threat than that presented by Syria and Ephraim. In fact, an opponent more powerful and devastating than the Syro-Ephraimitic coalition is waiting on the horizon to bring havoc to Judah.

3. *The Downfall of Judah* (7:17—8:18). Having rejected the opportunity to respond in faith, Ahaz chose a way which would cost the nation dearly.

(a) THE SHAVING OF JUDAH (7:17-25). Isaiah told Ahaz that his rejection of the sign placed the nation in its gravest danger since the days of the division of the kingdom in 931 B.C. (7:17). Yahweh will call forth the Egyptians and the Assyrians upon Judah (7:18), Isaiah informed him. They will come forth as flies and bees, who cannot be denied access to the rugged valleys and the clefts in the rocks as well as the wildest areas seldom seen by man — the place of thorn-hedges and bushes (7:19). There will be no defense which man might erect to prevent their overrunning the country.

After characterizing the nature of the encounter with Egypt and Assyria, the prophet continued his description of Judah's demise by concentrating on the activity of the Assyrians. The razor (Assyria), which Ahaz had hired to humiliate Syria and Ephraim, would in the end shave Judah (7:20). Shaving the body was an act of unspeakable indignity. So the point made by Isaiah was that the nation will be as humiliated by coming events as a man was when he was shaved. The once great agricultural nation will return to a pastoral existence. The population will be so depleted that there will be an abundance of those things which are produced with little, if any, human effort, butter and honey (7:21, 22). In the devastation to come, a thousand vines worth a thousand silver shekels (approximately $350.00) will be overgrown with briars and thorns (7:23). The cultivated areas will be so grown over that they will be good for nothing but hunting (7:24); the hills, usually cultivated with the mattock, will be so impassable and untillable that only cattle and sheep will frequent them (7:25). Ahaz, who had chosen the way of Assyria over "the sign," will become the victim of the one he had chosen.

(b) DARK CLOUDS ON JUDAH'S HORIZON (8:1-18). Isaiah now speaks a group of oracles which continue to develop the theme of the tragedy of Judah (8:1-18). 8:14 introduces the second son of Isaiah, Maher-shalal-hash-baz. The name of this son means "speed the spoil, hasten the booty," and, as suggested above, most scholars believe that his name was prophetic of the approaching destruction of the members of the Syro-Ephraimitic coalition (8:4). Having been made aware of the overthrow of her enemies by the sign of the son of Isaiah, the nation was charged with having "refused the waters of Shiloah" (8:6), that is, they did not trust in the provisions of Yahweh. So the waters of destruction by Assyria were to reach to Judah's neck but not go above it. Though there will not be a complete destruction, the waters would reach such a great depth that they would threaten the very life of the nation (8:8b).

Then the figure changes from the flood to that of the "outstretched wings" (8:8c). This has been interpreted as a figurative reference to the wings of Yahweh extended as protection over the land. The picture is one of Immanuel overshadowing His own, and, it may find support in the fact that the land was called "thy land, O Immanuel." If this is a valid approach to the passage, then it refers back to 7:14 in which Immanuel was promised for a time of need. That time was the Assyrian threat and Immanuel will protect His people and deliver them from the flood of the Assyrians.

After making the flood reference, the prophet described the folly of the nations taking counsel together (8:9, 10). Their counsel would come to nothing. The nations are no more than instruments which Yahweh uses for His own purposes — one the chastening of Judah — and when He is finished with them, they will "be broken in pieces" (8:9). Their counsel will end in utter failure because Yahweh was with His own to protect them (8:10b). Therefore, the people of Yahweh cannot be utterly destroyed. The flood was going to reach only to the country's neck (8:8).

These were times of crisis. There was a right way to act at such times and a wrong way. In 8:11-15 Isaiah was told what his duties were during such an era. His instructions came "with a strong hand," that is, they were words which could not be taken lightly. Isaiah was told to disassociate himself from the attitudes and purposes of the nation and declare that the one to fear and dread was Yahweh, not Assyria (8:12, 13). The prophet was told to sanctify Yahweh, and He would in turn be his sanctuary, security (8:14). But for those who refused to sanctify Him, Yahweh will become "a stone of stumbling and . . . a rock of offence" (8:14b). This verse foretells the appearance in Judah of a group who were to be no longer identified with the nation. It foretells the appearance of a group faithful to Yahweh and secure in Him. They were to be the core of the new nation.

In the meantime Isaiah was to "bind . . . up the testimony, seal the law among my disciples" (8:16) and await Yahweh's performance of His words (8:17). While they waited, Isaiah and his children were going to be around to constantly remind the people of "the signs" and "wonders" which Yahweh had already announced (8:18).

4. *The Contrast Between the Present Conditions and the Future Messianic Age* (8:19—9:7). Continuing with the contrast between a faithful group and an unfaithful one, Isaiah began this section by contrasting the character of true religion with that of false religion (8:19-22).

(a) THE FUTILITY OF FALSE RELIGION (8:19-22). False religion seeks counsel from the "familiar spirits" (perhaps a reference to the disembodied dead) and "the wizards" who practice the occult sciences. These counselors were referred to as chirpers and mutterers. They made these strange noises either to invoke their deities to respond, or to impart their messages (8:19). The people of Yahweh should not seek Him among the dead (8:19b). They should seek Him that they might live. They will find Him as they turn to "the law" for instruction and "the testimony" or witness of the prophet for the knowledge of the will of God (8:20). Those who forsake the true worship of Yahweh for false forms of religion will find themselves forsaken. Their privations and sufferings will cause them to fret themselves and curse their king and God, because their king was unable to relieve them and their God was not going to relieve them (8:21). They were going to be left without hope as they "turn their faces upward," heavenward. Heaven itself will offer them no hope and they will find nothing but darkness and despair as they "look unto the earth" (8:21c, 22). What a high price they must pay for having chosen a false way of worship over the true worship of Yahweh.

(b) The Light of the Messianic Age (9:1-7). In sharp contrast with the darkened condition found in 8:22, the prophet in 9:1-7 described the condition of light which was to come. The future was going to bring a difference in the conditions of Zebulun and Naphtali. They had been made subject to Assyria in 733 B.C. but they were going to be restored to a status more glorious than any enjoyed in the past (9:1). Their new condition will be based upon the fact that the darkness, and all the destructiveness associated with it, will be replaced by the light which inaugurates a new era of life, joy, and peace (9:2, 3). That new era will be preceded by the otherthrow of all their oppressors. They will be as completely routed as the Midianites, who had been permanently overthrown by Gideon and his army (v. 4). Even the Midianites recognized their defeat as the work of Yahweh (Judges 7:14). Then an era of peace in which every vestige of war is removed will be ushered in (9:5).

The future will not only be a time of peace, Isaiah told the people of Judah, it will also be an era of joy. The "yoke of burden" will be lifted and the "rod" and "staff" used by a tyrannical master will be broken (9:4). When these things come to pass, joy like that found at the harvest festival, or comparable to that manifest by soldiers gathering to divide the spoils of war, were going to break forth (9:3).

All those things which the prophet announced for the era of light, that is, deliverance, joy, and peace, were to be realized in the

'irth of a child (9:6). This child called "a son" is more than "a
gn" as in 7:14. He will be for their benefit, the people were
'ld. Isaiah was saying that "unto *us* a child is born . . . a son is
given" and the benefits from this One will be realized in His universal rule. He will be ruler in the total realm of nature as well as in
the spiritual realm (9:6a). He is to be called "a Wonder of a Coun-
selor." He is to bear this name because the counsel which He gives
will be above the counsel of ordinary men. It will be the counsel of
Yahweh, and therefore wonderful (cf. Isaiah 28:29). He is also to
be called "Mighty God," that is, "God of a Hero." All scholars do
not agree, but this title may refer to the pioneering nature of the
work of the child. If so, He will inaugurate a new thing in the
world. That new thing is the rule of Yahweh based upon true
righteousness.

The third title to be worn by the child is Father of Eternity. This
refers to the endlessness of His rule and the beneficent acts which
He performs on behalf of those under His rule. That is, Yahweh
will do for His own for an eternity what an earthly father would do
for his children as long as he lived.

The final title to be given "the child" is "Prince of Peace." The
name refers to the fact that wherever and whenever He ruled there
will be peace.

Having announced the titles to be borne by "the child," Isaiah
concluded the section by describing the extent and character of the
kingdom which He is to establish. It will be an everlasting kingdom
which furnishes an unending peace for its citizenry and which is
distinguished by its justice and righteousness (9:7). The prospect
of such a kingdom must have challenged the capacity of Isaiah's
hearers. Undoubtedly, there were those who had reservations about
the possibility of such a remarkable thing coming to pass. Therefore, as though the prophet had anticipated the skepticism of
his hearers, he declared how it would be brought about: "the zeal
of Jehovah of hosts will perform this" (9:7c). Since this was not the
work of man but of Yahweh, it could not be denied its full realization.

5. *Imminent Judgment Upon Ephraim* (9:8—10:4). The
prophecy contained in this section is believed to have been composed sometime before the beginning of the Syro-Ephraimitic War
(*ca.* 735 B.C.). It describes the conditions in Israel at that time.
The spirit of the nation was displayed by the proud, greedy, and

immoral people living in a false sense of security. Because of this condition, Isaiah revealed that the word which the Lord had sent against Jacob (Israel) would "light" upon the nation in the form of judgment (9:8, 9). The proud nation, even in face of the threat posed by the united effort of the Syrians and Ephraim, persuaded herself that if destruction were to come she could quickly replace all that she lost (9:10). Such pride could not go unchallenged. Therefore Yahweh was going to raise up adversaries who will devour Israel's territory as completely as wild beasts devour a prey (9:11, 12). The people were not going to repent (9:13). Therefore a more severe judgment will follow. The leaders ("head") as well as their followers ("tail") will be cut off (9:14, 15), the leaders because they led astray and the followers because they allowed themselves to be led astray (9:16). Even the widow and the orphan were not to receive mercy at Yahweh's hands, so bad were the conditions (9:17). Such strong language suggests the total rejection of the nation by Yahweh. There were not going to be enough left in the future for the young men to dream of the day when they could lead and be responsible (9:17a).

The last paragraph in chapter nine describes the judgment of Yahweh. It is characterized as a fire sent to consume "the people . . . as the fuel of fire" (9:19). The inhabitants of Judah, whose wickedness "burneth as a fire . . . devoureth the briars and thorns . . ." (9:18a), would themselves be declared fuel for the fire of Yahweh's judgment. A nation so filled with cruelty, jealousy, and inhumanity could expect no less (9:19c, 20).

Finally, Isaiah discussed those who wrote briefs and rendered judgments which thwarted justice and caused it to fail (10:1, 2). These along with the others were to come under the wrath of Yahweh (10:3). Should they flee to their false gods for help, it would be in vain (10:4). There will not be a secure place. All avenues will be dead ends and, instead of delaying His judgment, such vain attempts will only encourage it (10:4b).

6. *The Prophetic View of History* (10:5-34). At the time of Isaiah's ministry, Assyria was the dominant world power. Every nation in that part of the world had been, or would in time be, affected by the aggressive tendencies of this great empire. In the eyes of the world Assyria appears to be beyond the limits of all control. But Isaiah's eyes saw things differently.

(a) THE ROD IN YAHWEH'S HAND (10:5-19). Isaiah saw the

Assyrians as nothing more than a rod in the hands of Yahweh by which He metes out His judgment upon the nations (10:5). Assyria, without knowing it, was being used to cut off nations deserving Yahweh's judgment. They thought their policies were going to further their own ends (10:6, 7). They had met with remarkable success and had taken all the credit for it. Such a philosophy of history naturally encouraged boastfulness and drove them on to one reckless pursuit after another (10:8-11). They even dreamed of the day that they would occupy the Holy City itself (10:11). Such personal vaunting was blasphemy and did not go unnoticed by Yahweh. So He told Isaiah that when Assyria came near to Jerusalem it was because He had allowed it (10:12). No room was to remain for the proud boasting of Assyria because she had been but the instrument of His judgment. Before He had finished with her, leanness and death will have come upon her fat, expensively equipped army (10:16, 17). There will be so few left after Yahweh — the "light of Israel" and "his Holy One" — finishes His destruction that a small child will be able to count them (10:18, 19).

This entire section (10:5-19) reflects Isaiah's view of history. Instead of seeing a world in which nations run rampant at will to accomplish their own ends, Isaiah saw a sovereign God so much in control of personal and international events that even the wicked could be used to serve His purposes. He was not implying that God directed Assyria in her evil plans, only that He did turn her evil plans to serve His own purpose. Then, as though to teach the Assyrians that they were still responsible for their plans, He revealed that they too were to be judged according to the same righteous standards by which Israel and Judah have been judged. They will suffer just as much at the hand of Yahweh for allowing themselves to be used to mete out His judgment as those who suffered His judgment at their hands.

Certainly this worthy concept of history contains a message for every generation of men. It teaches all nations that there is a sovereign God who is above history, but who works in and through history. To experience long life a nation must abide in His will. To refuse to conform to His purposes of righteousness will bring destruction, regardless of the nature and number of resources held by that nation. Though a nation opposed to the revealed will of God may find itself an instrument in His hand, as did Assyria, it will not stand. It will be judged like every nation opposed to God and His purpose.

(b) A MESSAGE OF CONSOLATION (10:20-34). These words of consolation predict the return of the remnant made up of those who had repented and turned to Yahweh (10:21). They were to become the recipients of His sure promise (10:20). Though the people of Israel were as numerous "as the sand of the sea," Isaiah stated that after the destruction "only a remnant of them shall return" (10:22). Those not turning to Yahweh were to be destroyed by that which He was about to execute "in the midst of the land" (10:23).

A section (10:24-27) follows which was addressed to Jerusalem. The city was advised not to fear the Assyrians, even though they lift up their staff against the city (10:24). In "a very little while" Yahweh will stir up a scourge against them which will bring about the complete relief of the nation (10:26, 27). Such words must have brought great comfort to the hearts of those who heard them.

The last section (10:28-34) is a description of the approach of the Assyrian army under Sennacherib in 701 B.C. and Yahweh's ultimate destruction of the Assyrians. The Assyrians were depicted as approaching Jerusalem from the north. In fact, the cities mentioned were all to the north of Jerusalem. In the case of Michmash, there was a narrow pass which required the army to store its baggage and other sizeable objects before it could slip through the limited passageway (10:28-31).

Verses 33 and 34 suggest the complete destruction of the Assyrians. Though there is not general agreement here, and some even suggest that the prophecy was one announced upon Israel and Judah, it seems that the context favors the destruction of Assyria. Nevertheless, the destruction was to be as total as that left by the forester who had completed cutting down the trees and clearing out the undergrowth.

7. *The Establishment of the Messiah's Kingdom* (11:1—12:6). In sharp contrast with the destruction of Assyria in 10:33, 34, Isaiah portrayed the future of Judah and Jerusalem. If the previous passage (10:33, 34) referred to the destruction of Assyria, then it was for the purpose of emphasizing the difference between the future of Assyria and that of Judah and Jerusalem.

(a) THE ADVENT OF THE MESSIAH (11:1-10). A sprout or branch would ". . . shoot out of the stock of Jesse, and . . . shall bear fruit" (1:1). This was the prophet's way of saying that from Jesse, David's father, a son would appear.

The appearance of "Jesse's son" means the restoration of the Davidic dynasty. When this One comes He will be endowed with "the Spirit of Jehovah" (11:2). This "Spirit" brings intellectual gifts as well as practical and religious ones, which enable Him to accomplish the purpose which Yahweh had for Him. The "Spirit of Yahweh," referred to as the "Holy Spirit" in Psalm 51 and in the New Testament, is the agent which enables the accomplishing of God's purpose by one commissioned to perform a special work. In this case the scion of Jesse was to reign as Messiah (11:3-5). His delight was to be in His dedication to Yahweh. He was to hold Him in awesome reverence, and because of this, His standard for judging will be righteousness (11:4). When He comes to reign, and where He reigns, there will be no bartering at the market place of justice. Every judgment will be made on the basis of truth and honor (11:4) and He will smite those who take advantage of the poor and meek (11:5). His very dress will be "righteousness" and "faithfulness" (11:5).

Since the Messiah will rule in righteousness and truth, the people could expect changed conditions in the place of His rule. These conditions are stated in 11:6-9. There will be a complete transformation of the world of nature as well as of the world of the spirit. In the idealized conditions of the age to come, the prophet saw the abolition of all natural hostility and killing. It will be a time when all the world will be at peace because the sovereign is the Prince of Peace. It will be a time when there will be no more evil. The earth will be as "full of the knowledge of Jehovah as the waters cover the sea," that is, it will have certain knowledge of His rule in love and obedience (11:9).

In that day, when "the root of Jesse" appears, He will stand as an ensign. He will serve as a rallying point around which men will be united in the common knowledge that He rules in righteousness and effects changes which cause men to live in righteousness. At that time, "his resting place" — the place of His rule will "be glorious" (11:10).

(b) ISRAEL IN THE NEW AGE (11:11-16). With the conditions of the new age set forth, the prophet discussed Israel in that age (11:11-16). Since there seems to be a break in the continuity of the chapter between 11:10 and 11 some have suggested that the material may have come from different periods in the prophet's ministry. But the argument that this would be the natural point for the prophet to consider the role of Israel in the new age is stronger.

The new age for Israel will see the remnant returned to the land from every corner of the earth (11:11, 12). Every impediment to their restoration will have been overcome. Examples of the extent of the preparation for them are seen in the destruction of "the tongue of the Egyptian sea," a figure for the Gulf of Suez, and in the dividing of the River, the Euphrates or the Nile, that these would no longer be hindrances to those returning to the land (11:15). There will be a highway from Assyria which they will travel with the same assurance that Israel had known at the first when she "came up out of the land of Egypt" (11:16, cf. 11:11a).

Yet there will be things accomplished in the restoration of the remnant that were not necessary in the Exodus. This time there will be the need to heal the breach between Israel and Judah which occurred in 931 B.C., as well as the necessity of gathering the remnants of both nations from their places of deportation (11:12, 13). Both of these have great significance for the people of God. They will be restored into the purpose of Yahweh and also be provided with sufficient strength to move as a great bird "upon the shoulder" (coastline) to destroy their enemies on the west, as well as despoil those on the east of their vast riches. Through these triumphs their enemies will be brought under the domination of the unified people of the restoration (11:14).

(c)  A SONG OF THANKSGIVING (12:1-6). As the conclusion of this great section on the restoration there appears, and very appropriately, a song of thanksgiving which has two stanzas (12:1-2 and 12:3-6). The first stanza appears to be an expression of the prophet's thanksgiving. Rather naturally, he lifts his voice in thanksgiving for the fact that Yahweh has turned the expressions of His anger into words of comfort (12:1). Yahweh has again proven that He is the source of salvation (12:2). In face of the threat of the Assyrians, these words were expressing the conviction that though God allows the chastening and purifying of the nation, there will be a future deliverance (salvation). It will be the work of Yahweh who is their "strength" (protection) and "song" (the object of praise). With Yahweh's deliverance there will be nothing to fear, thus the words, ". . . I will trust and will not be afraid . . ." (12:2).

The second part of the song (12:3-6) reflects a less personal expression of thanksgiving and contains words of admonition. Verse 3, which seems to serve as a prelude, characterizes the salvation to be experienced. It will be a source of unspeakable joy comparable to that of the weary, parched traveler in the desert who comes upon a spring of water. His joy overwhelms him. Just as such a person rejoices in coming upon a perpetual stream, so the remnant will rejoice in the wells of salvation. The salvation of Yahweh will be in unending supply. When men realize it, there will be every reason to give thanks to Him and declare the greatness of what He has done.

As a result of these responses on the part of those who experience deliverance, they will declare: ". . . his name is exalted" (12:4). Yahweh had done excellent things. His people — the inhabitants of Zion (12:6) — were delivered. Therefore, it would be right that there should be singing of praises and crying aloud with shouting in order that the world might know of His glorious works (12:5, 6).

## FOR FURTHER STUDY OR DISCUSSION

1. Read article on "Rezin" in IDB, Volume IV, p. 74 and ZPBD, p. 722.

2. Read article on "Pekah" in IDB, Volume III, p. 708 and ZPBD, p. 632.

3. Read article on "Virgin" in IDB, Volume IV, pp. 787, 788 and in ZPBD, p. 882.

4. Read article on "Ahaz" in IDB, Volume I, pp. 64-66 and ZPBD, p. 23.

5. Is it possible for decisions made today to have such extended consequence as the one made by Ahaz in Isaiah 7? What might these decisions be? Who makes such decisions today?

6. Does God still use the enemies of His people and purpose to chastise His own people? In addition to the example in Isaiah 10:5 ff., what other cases do you consider to be similar? Why?

7. Is it possible to have peace in the world? If not, why not? If so, under what conditions? Is it possible without "the Prince of Peace"? If so, how? What do you personally believe?

8. Under what conditions will the world know the peace described in Isaiah 11:6-9?

9. What is the relationship between "the Messianic Age" and "the latter days"? When did or will, as the case may be, the latter days begin? Does one's belief on this matter affect his theology? How?

# CHAPTER 4

# Jehovah and the Staff of the Wicked

(Isaiah 13-23)

Chapter thirteen begins a new direction in the book of Isaiah. The nations who had been the enemies of Yahweh and His people are now brought under condemnation (cf. Amos 1-2; Jeremiah 46-51 and Ezekiel 25-32.) Not only is the demise of the nations important, a profound theological concept is emphasized. Yahweh is sovereign of all the earth! This was a doctrine that Israel and Judah needed to comprehend if they were ever to understand the significance of the events in their own lives. As they were subdued by and then delivered from one nation after the other, they needed to see the all-encompassing purpose of Yahweh. Isaiah pointed this out as he announced judgment upon nation after nation. This was not the first time he had stated this truth. In 10:5 ff., the prophet clearly saw the sovereign God of the universe using an enemy, the Assyrians, as a rod to chasten his own people. Then He broke the staff of the very nation He had used because it had permitted itself to be worked with for such an ignominious purpose. The nations were to be judged by earth's sovereign, and because of it Israel and Judah were to take heart. They would be restored after the fall of their enemies. Yahweh's plan for Israel and Judah could not be thwarted.

Largely on the basis of what has been called "historical evidence," many scholars have claimed that Isaiah did not write chapters thirteen to twenty-three. Their reasoning is based on the historical position of Babylon when Isaiah was preaching and writing: (1) Assyria, not Babylon, was the greatest power in the world. Isaiah's description of Babylonian supremacy antedated the historical occurrence by approximately one hundred years. (2) The Babylonians and the Medes were allies, not enemies, during Isaiah's time. (3) The Medes were the cause of Babylon's downfall, sure enough, but this happened after the beginning of the sixth century B.C. — a fact that Isaiah could not have known.

There are those, equally insistent, who believe that Isaiah did write these passages and that they refer to events which occured in the future. He himself indicates this in 13:1. They believe that the prophet learned of the events in visions from God. They do not deny the truth of what the others say; instead they establish an explanation for it. To do more than state both sides of the argument would be to go beyond the scope of this study guide.

1. *The Fall of Babylon* (13:1—14:23). The prophet opened the section given to the foreign prophecies by announcing judgment upon Babylon and her king. Instructions were given to display a banner upon a mountain, which had been denuded of all trees, in order that all Yahweh's warriors (consecrated ones — the Medes) might see it and make preparation to enter the gates of Babylon (13:1, 3). Immediately the prophet heard the noise of the movement of the multitudes (Medes) mustering for the conflict (13:4). They began their advance toward Babylon under their "general" Yahweh (13:5), and it was announced that the day of Jehovah was at hand (13:6). This announcement struck terror, despair, and horror into the hearts of those about to receive the brunt of the blow (13:7, 8).

The announcement of judgment is followed by a section which details the results of that judgment (13:9-16). According to the prophet it was going to be a day of utter darkness (13:10; cf. Amos

5:18) in which the whole land will be made a desolation and its occupants will be destroyed (13:9). Through such action Yahweh will purge the land. Destruction will fall upon the wicked, arrogant, and terrible occupants of Babylon (13:11). In that day, human life will be as scarce as fine gold, even scarcer than the gold from the city of Ophir in South Arabia, renowned for an exceptional quality of gold (13:12). The force of that day of judgment was going to be so devastating that the heavens and the earth will be shaken to their foundations (13:13). Nothing will be exempt from Yahweh's wrath. Even the foreigners, who had been attracted by Babylon's wealth, will flee to their homelands to escape. All who fail to escape will be slain along with the Babylonians, their children dashed to pieces, their homes plundered, and their wives ravished (13:14-16). This overthrow will be brought about by Yahweh's instrument, the Medes, who could not be bought off by the Babylonians (13:17, 18). Babylon will be so devastated that it will be a habitat for wild beasts (13:20-22), Isaiah reported. She will be left as Yahweh had left Sodom and Gomorrah on another day of judgment (13:19, cf. Genesis 19:24-28).

In association with Babylon's destruction will come the deliverance of the house of Israel and a complete about-face in circumstances. Whereas the people of Israel had been the servants of the Babylonians, the Babylonians will become subject to Israel and minister to her as servants and handmaids (14:1, 2).

In this day, the day of restoration, related to the Messianic Age in the prophetic scheme of things, those restored will take up a "parable" or "taunt-song" with which to describe the descent of the king of Babylon into Sheol — the abode of the dead.

The song begins with a description of the destruction of Babylon's power (14:4b-8). The interjections of verse 4 show the astonishment which characterized the people in face of the demise of the powerful king of Babylon (14:4b).

The picture is that of God's breaking the rod used to afflict His people as well as the scepter of the tyrants who ruled them (14:5). When this happens the whole earth, free from the continuing anger and oppressive power of Babylon, will break forth with singing (14:6, 7). Nature herself will rejoice, since the trees of Lebanon need no longer be cut down and borne away to Babylon to be made into palaces (14:8).

In sharp contrast to "the rest and quiet" of earth, Sheol will come alive with activity as it awaits the coming of the king of

Babylon (14:9). The dead rulers already in Sheol wait expectantly for his arrival (14:9b). None of them can believe that this great ruler could come to their state (14:10). The pompous, extravagant ruler will be denied the splendor of his banqueting and reveling. In place of the luxurious carpets upon which he walked in the palace, he will find worms; rather than elegant covers, there will be worms which will eat away at his flesh (14:11).

The fall of the ruler, described by interjection, was compared to the fall of one of the minor star deities who sought to ascend above the throne of God. This could never be allowed because heaven could tolerate but one ruler (14:12-14). So because of his presumption and severity, the proud ruler must be brought to the very bottom of the pit (Sheol). The deeper in Sheol he is, the more hopeless the condition of the offender and the greater the affliction. There is no escape from the bottom (14:15). What an ignoble end for one once so powerful and exalted!

Verses 16-19 shift to the field of battle in which the king will lose his life. There the victors will gaze upon the dead king and marvel at his overthrow (14:16, 17). Whereas kings were customarily buried in the family sepulcher, the burial of the king of Babylon compares to that of a son who had been disinherited (14:18, 19a). His remains left on the field of battle will be piled over with stones ("the stones of the pit") (14:19). There will be a complete end to the empire of the evil king. His seed, "the seed of evildoers," will never again occupy the throne — "shall not be named forever" (14:20). They will be destroyed (14:21). Then, after the distressful picture of destruction in verse 21, an epilogue follows which reflects back to chapter thirteen and generalizes the destructive action of Yahweh (14:22, 23).

2. *Judgment Upon Assyria and Philistia* (14:24-32). The remainder of chapter fourteen (14:24-32) consists of two paragraphs, one concerning Assyria and the other Philistia. The first states Yahweh's intention to destroy the Assyrians in the land of promise (14:24-27). The second contains His warning to the Philistines. They are not to rejoice over the death of an oppressive Assyrian ruler. Another enemy is going to appear, close on the Assyrian's heels, to carry out God's judgment (14:28-31). Yet while these disasters befall them, Zion will be secure in God's protection (14:32).

3. *The Devastation of the Land of Moab* (15:1—16:14). An

announcement of judgment on Moab undoubtedly brought rejoicing to those who heard the prophet. Moab, like the other nations, had been a long-time enemy of Israel and Judah (cf. Numbers 22-24 and Judges 3:14 ff.). Because of her evil ways, Yahweh will bring an end to Moab. In the night, suddenly, the land will be brought to nothing. From Ar of Moab (located to the north on the Arnon River) to Kir of Moab (south of Ar) there will be nothing but waste and destruction (15:1). Desolation, destruction, and weeping will grip the country from border to border (15:2-9). The Moabite's humiliation will be complete for they would have to cut their hair and wear sackcloth (15:2-3). The condition of the inhabitants will be so pitiable, and the heartbreak of those attempting to escape, so severe, that Isaiah's heart went out to them (15:5).

Chapter 16:1-5 contains a desperate appeal by the Moabites to Judah for justice and righteousness. With the tribute of lambs, the scattered refugees seek protection ("thy shade as the night") and a dwelling place in Judah (16:1-4). Upon their arrival, they will submit themselves to the reign of David in a kingdom founded on the principles of justice and righteousness (16:5).

Immediately the account of the severity of Moab's devastation is resumed (16:6-12). Because of her pride and boasting, Moab will be so completely razed that all the vines will be destroyed and there will be no more raisin cakes for the religious feasts (16:7, 8). The country so stripped of vines will provoke bitter weeping from the inhabitants (16:9, 10), and the severity of the destruction again moved Isaiah to join in the weeping (16:11). This loss will bring the people to their place of prayer where they beseech their gods for deliverance, but with no response (16:12).

The last paragraph of chapter sixteen reveals that God had spoken to Moab previously and that she was without excuse (16:13). Therefore, within three years, a period no longer than that in which a man wishes to hire out (and he does so for as short a time as possible), Moab will be brought into contempt. Just a remnant will remain (16:14).

4. *The Overthrow of Damascus and Ephraim* (17:1-14). Isaiah next turned to pronounce words of judgment upon the nations of the Syro-Ephraimitic coalition (17:1-3). Damascus will be left a "ruinous heap" and Ephraim will lose her fortification. The reference to Ephraim's fortification may have been to the defense which Syria offered Ephraim as she joined her on her territory, thereby upgrad-

ing Ephraim's; or it may have been simply a reference to Samaria, in whose destruction the fortification of Ephraim would for all practical purposes be lost.

When the judgment comes to pass, the glory of Ephraim (all that she boasted in: people, military strength and great wealth) will disappear as weight from a fat person (17:4). Then, instead of her wealth, strength, and beauty, there will be impoverishment, weakness, and ugliness. The population of Israel will be as thoroughly cut off as the quality grain of the valley of Rephaim when gathered by the reaper (17:5). With that same thoroughness the reaper will pass through Jacob, only in this case it is not because of her value but because of her worthlessness. Yet, despite every caution in gathering the crop, there were always those corners and other areas left for the gleaner (See Leviticus 19:9 ff.; 23:22 and Deuteronomy 24: 19-21). Similarly, Yahweh will leave a few survivors in Ephraim. They are compared to the few olives left in the top of the tree after the reaper had gathered the fruit (17:6). Even though that few remained, the harvest will be considered complete.

As a result of the judgment, Israel, who had forgotten her God, will have so learned her lesson that she will look to Yahweh and cease depending upon man and his creations (17:7-9). She will have learned the futility of seeking the favor of the gods by planting gardens in their honor, because even this will bring nothing but "grief and desperate sorrow" (17:10, 11).

The final paragraph of chapter seventeen refers to the mustering of the nations to carry out their own designs. The passage may have been a reference to the Syrians, the Assyrians, or even Israel. Whatever the point of reference, the passage teaches that even though they are as strong as raging flood waters Yahweh will scatter them as the chaff and blown dust (17:13). The point is, those who spoiled and robbed and defied the purpose of Yahweh will be brought to nothing, whoever they might be (17:14).

5. *The Prophetic Message to Ethiopia* (18:1-7). This prophecy, like many of the others in Isaiah, had to do with the destruction of the Assyrians. Ambassadors had been sent to Jerusalem from Ethiopia, a land of locusts and grasshoppers ("land of the rustling of wings"), to enlist the support of Judah in a rebellion against Assyria (18:1, 2). Isaiah, who had opposed Ahaz's turning to Assyria, also objected to the idea of a union with Ethiopia. So, he told the ambassadors to return home and await the lifting up of the ensign

on the mountains and the blowing of the trumpet (18:3). He meant
these as instructions to await the moment of Yahweh's call to battle.
As just after the dew and heat of the sun there was the time of
harvest, so will there be a proper time for the cutting down of the
Assyrians (18:5). When that day arrives, the dead bodies of the
Assyrians will litter the fields of battle and will be left as carrion
for the birds and beasts (18:6). Then upon the knowledge of the
overthrow of the Assyrian power, the Ethiopians will bring gifts of
homage to Yahweh who had devastated the Assyrians (18:7). From
afar they would come bearing gifts "to the place of the name
of Jehovah of hosts, the mount Zion."

6. *The Judgment of Yahweh on Egypt* (19:1-25). Though
there are differing opinions concerning the relationship between 19:
1-15 and 19:18-25, perhaps the best approach is to look upon the
first divison as the picture of Egypt's judgment. Verses 16 and 17
serve as a transition between the two sections, and 18-25 refer to
the time that the Egyptians would look to Yahweh.

The first section (19:1-4), having to do with judgment upon
Egypt, depicts Yahweh riding upon the clouds — perhaps describing
a storm — and bringing despair upon the Egyptian gods and people
(19:1). There will be nothing but anarchy in the land (19:2).
Any comfort the people might expect from their religious practices
— idolatry, soothsaying, ghost worship or turning to familiar spirits
— will not materialize (19:3). In spite of all their gods, the Egyptians will still fall under the rule of a cruel Assyrian monarch (19:
4). The reference may have been to one of two Assyrian rulers:
Esar-Haddon or Ashurbanipal. It is known that both overran the
Egyptians, Esar-Haddon in 672 B.C. and Ashurbanipal ten years
later.

The conditions pictured in Egypt at the time imply more than
simply a conquest by the Assyrians (19:5-10). The vivid language
describing a natural disaster, the drying up of the Nile and the
stench of other streams as the water vanished, suggest a severe
drought coinciding with the Assyrian conquest (19:5). A drought
will make farming and fishing impossible (19:6-8). As a result,
the pillars (leaders) of the nation will be unable to solve the problem
and anguish of unemployment; "all they that work for hire shall be
grieved in soul" (19:10). The prophet was saying that all industries including the major ones of weaving, farming, and fishing

would be shut down as a result of the drought. A picture of utter dejection for the Egyptians!

The circumstances resulting from these disasters will completely confound the princes and the wise men of Egypt (19:11-15). They will not be able to declare Yahweh's plan for Egypt (19:12b). He will have so confused them by His acts (19:14) that not one of them, leader or follower, will know what to do to stabilize conditions (19:15). The entire population will be as helpless and as faint-hearted as the women (19:16). In that day, Judah, so long domi-nated and mocked by the Egyptians, will become a terror for them (19:17). In Egypt there will be set up five Hebrew colonies which speak the language of Canaan and worship Yahweh of hosts (19:18). One of the cities will be called "the City of the Sun," "the City of Righteousness," or "the City of Destruction" — which of these translations is preferable is uncertain. It may be that the three translations reflect the history of the name of one of the cities. It was perhaps originally known as "the City of Righteousness," until it came to be called "the City of the Sun." If this is so, then in all likelihood the third name, "the City of Destruction," may have been its final name. The city may have been called this to disassociate it from Jerusalem or to show the disdain the orthodox community had for Egypt.

If the city mentioned in 19:18 was at one time referred to as "the City of Righteousness," it seems likely that this city will be the one to erect an altar to Jehovah (19:19). Involved in building an altar is setting up a boundary stone on the border of Egypt either to designate it as a possession of Yahweh or to declare that Yahweh was known there. As a result of their knowledge of Yahweh (if it were the knowledge of experience) the Egyptians will call upon Him and He will deliver them from their Assyrian oppressors just as He had promised to deliver Israel and Judah. But such a de-liverance can only occur when they know and worship Yahweh (19:21). Then if they violate His purpose, they will know "the Grace of Smiting" and be healed through the judgment of Yahweh, thereby being restored to His favor (19:22).

In the day that Yahweh will be known, the archenemies, Egypt and Assyria, will make peace with each other and will worship together (19:23). Joining with Israel, they will be united in the kingdom of God (19:25). Israel will still maintain the distinction of being Jehovah's in that they are the only ones to wear the name "inheritance." Nevertheless, Egypt and Assyria will be the work of

His hands and a part of His purpose. What a day of miracles that will be!

7. *The Conquest of Egypt and Ethiopia* (20:1-6). The context of chapter twenty is the Ashdod Rebellion of 711 B.C. The invasion of Ashdod was to overthrow those forces that threatened a revolt against Assyria. Sargon sent his commander in chief "who fought against Ashdod and took it" (20:1). Isaiah received instructions from Yahweh that he was to walk about Jerusalem naked (with only his loincloth and with bare feet) for a period of three years (714-711 B.C.?) in order to impress upon Judah the end result of rebelling against Assyria. He was acting out the consequences of the rebellion, saying that the Egyptians and Ethiopians will be led away naked and barefoot into Assyria (20:3, 4).

Judah will be overwhelmed by what has happened to her potential allies (20:5), and the pro-Egyptian faction in Judah will realize the folly of an attempt to lead the nation to join with the rebels. With the defeat of Ashdod, the coastland, Philistia and Judah, will recognize the futility of seeking deliverance from the domination of Assyria (20:6).

8. *The Fate of Babylon, Edom, and Arabia* (21:1-17). The oracles concerning Babylon, Edom, and Arabia are most difficult to interpret. The first, found in verses 1-10, deals with the conquest of Babylon by the Persians. The chapter opens with an unusual heading the "burden of the wilderness of the sea," which may have been an attempt to identify Babylon as the nation which was at one time a sea and which would again become a part of the sea (21:1a). If this is the proper meaning of the sentence, then the return to the sea is a figure of the results of the whirlwind advance of the Persian armies against Babylon (21:1). Thus, the vision which the prophet had seen was a "grievous" (hard) one (21:2). It was a vision of plundering and destroying. The dominions of Cyrus, including both Elam and Media, will besiege the Babylonians. Only then will the sighings of the misery she had brought upon the world cease (21:2b).

Upon seeing the vision, the prophet was overcome with anguish and fear. His pains were compared to those of a woman in labor. They were so intense that he neither saw nor heard anything else (21:3). His mind ("heart") reeled, horror gripped him, and his hours of peaceful reflection turned to evenings of trembling (21:4). In sharp contrast, his picture of the Babylonians is of merry making:

"prepare the table, they set the watch, they eat, they drink . . ." In the midst of their banqueting, realizing that the enemy is without the gate, they will oil their shields (either to protect them from rust or to enhance their deflective capacity) in preparation for the battle (21:5).

Judah was given instructions to carry out during that time of horror for Babylon (6-10). A watchman was to be stationed to bring word if anyone approached the city (21:6, 7). After a watch of some length, the watchman will declare that the riders were approaching with the news that Babylon was fallen at last (21:8, 9). That good word will soon be declared to those who had been Babylon's "threshing, and the grain of [its] floor" (21:10). At last, oppressive Babylon will be no more.

The second division (verses 11, 12) of chapter 21 contains an oracle concerning Dumah. Dumah means "silence" in the original language and may therefore have been a play on the name Edom. The Septuagint reads Edom instead of Dumah, and some of the manuscripts have Edom in their margins, so the reference is undoubtedly to Edom. This interpretation is confirmed by the allusion to Seir which was often used as a reference to Edom. The reference may have been to the personal concern of Edom over the Assyrian threat to her trade routes. The concern expressed in the questions of verse 11 may simply reflect a desire to know when the threat will end. If this is so, then the response of the prophet suggests that the answer was uncertain. It was as though he were saying the future will hold both light and darkness, deliverance and affliction. Because of the indefinite answer, the inquirer is told to continue inquiring and perhaps in due time the answer will be clearer (21: 12).

The third division (verses 13-17) of chapter 21 contains an oracle concerning Arabia. The section opens with a picture of merchants from Dedan (near the north end of Akaba) being forced off their regular routes into the wilderness where they were left without access to food and water (21:13-15). Their only hope was in the generosity of the inhabitants of Tema (21:14).

Should the incident refer to an attempt by the Assyrians against the Arabians, the last section of the passage (21:16-17) may have the added meaning of the Assyrians' being the rod of Yahweh's wrath. Here was another occasion on which Yahweh would mete out judgment at the hands of the Assyrians.

9. *Judah's Day of Tumult and the Condemnation of Shebna*
(22:1-25). The prophecy opens with tumultuous rejoicing. The
occasion was the deliverance of Jerusalem from Sennacherib in
701 B.C. (II Kings 19). After that miraculous event the people
took to their housetops to celebrate (22:1, 2). It was an unparalleled occasion in the life of Judah. Although the people found
occasion for revelry, Isaiah saw none. It was a dark day for him.
The leaders had forsaken the people in the crisis and had sought
to escape without any thought of the welfare of the populace (22:3).
Such dereliction of duty on the part of the leaders and such pre-
mature rejoicing on the part of the people depressed the prophet to
the point of tears (22:4). He saw the occasion differently. He saw
ultimate judgment coming upon the nation — this was but a temporary reprieve (22:5). He saw the disaster which the city was
going to face. In the ultimate judgment the walls will be broken
down by the attacks of the enemy (22:5b, 6) and every "covering"
(defense) will fail the city (22:8). The enemy will occupy the
valleys around the city, and according to verse 7 will "set themselves in array at the gate." They will not be so readily turned
back as was Sennacherib. Although great precautions were to be
taken to secure the city with its water supply, they would be in vain.
The impending judgment was more than just the threat of another
army. It was the work of God. This the nation did not see but
this the prophet saw all too well (22:11b).

Judah, ignoring every warning, had interpreted events as oc-
casions for rejoicing. Isaiah interpreted them as calls to repentance
(22:12, 13). Since there was no repentance, there will be no
forgiveness. The result will be death (22:14).

After the gloomy picture of conditions in Judah both at that
time and in the future, the prophet delivered a condemnation of
Shebna, the prime minister (22:15-25). When Isaiah confronted
him, Shebna was evidently in the process of inspecting or directing
work on a tomb which was being built for him (22:16). Isaiah
declared, and for what reason it is not known, that Shebna will be
removed from office and banished from the land of Yahweh "into
a large country," that is, Assyria (22:18). There he will die without the glory accorded him in Judah. In Judah he rode in the
chariots, a sign of station, but in Assyria there will be no chariots
for him because there he will be just a foreigner (22:18b).

The office which Shebna had formerly held was to be given to
Eliakim (22:20, 21). From the description which follows, the posi-

tion evidently carried considerable authority (22:22-24). Eliakim will be given "the key of the house of David." This was a symbolic presentation which carried with it authority over everything and everyone in the king's household, with the exception of the royal family itself (22:22). Therefore his decisions will be final and he will be as "a father to the inhabitants of Jerusalem" (22:21). He will be both their adviser and protector.

Eliakim will display an otherwise obscure family upon "a throne of glory" (22:23, 24) in the same conspicuous way a person displays his utensils upon pegs in view of everyone. It is interesting to note that verse 24 refers to the most ordinary vessels. The implication may be that the family of Eliakim was not worthy of the potential honor, a suggestion which seems to be borne out by the fact that Eliakim will be cut off from office (22:25).

10. *The Burden of Tyre* (23:1-18). The last oracle delivered upon the nations was for Tyre. It is in two sections: Tyre's destruction (1-14), and Tyre's restoration (15-18).

The first division of the chapter describes the dismay created when word of the destruction of Tyre is made known. The ships from Tarshish (Spain) learn that Tyre has been destroyed at Kittim (Cyprus) (23:1). All the inhabitants of the coast (Phoenicia) are told to be dumb with shock (23:2). Those who had made their wealth upon trade from Shihor (the Nile) were no more (23:3). Egypt shudders at the news (23:4) and the population of Phoenicia is advised to flee to Tarshish (23:6). The once proud city is no more.

Then as though seeking to answer the queries of the citizens of Tyre and the world, the prophet revealed that this had been the work of Yahweh (23:8, 9). With the destruction of Tyre the inhabitants of Tarshish were as unrestrained as the Nile at the time of the flood (23:10). Yahweh had stretched out His hand and commanded that the strongholds and fortresses be destroyed (23:11). There would be no occasion for Tyre to rejoice (23:12) because all her strength had been destroyed (23:14). Yet after a lengthy period (seventy years) in eclipse, Tyre will sing as a harlot (23:15-16). She will sing because, after having been forgotten for so long a time, her lovers will approach her again. Tyre will again take up her profitable merchandising enterprises (23:17). Now, however, her wealth will be devoted to Yahweh and be used to sustain His people (23:18).

## For Further Study or Discussion

1. Is God still in control of the destiny of nations? If so, how has He demonstrated it in your lifetime? If not, why not?

2. Read article on "Babylon" in IDB, Volume I, pp. 334-338 and in ZPBD, pp. 89-93.

3. Read article on "Assyria and Babylonia" in IDB, Volume I, pp. 263-304 and the article on "Assyria" in ZPBD, pp. 78, 79.

4. Read article on "Syria" in ZPBD, pp. 820, 821.

5. Read article on "Egypt" in IDB, Volume II, pp. 39-66.

6. Read article on "Ethiopia" in ZPBD, pp. 262, 263 and IDB, Volume II, pp. 176, 177.

7. Read article on "Edom" in IDB, Volume II, pp. 24-26 and in ZPBD, pp. 233, 234.

8. Read article on "Tyre" in IDB, Volume IV, pp. 721-723.

9. Read article on "Arabia" in IDB, Volume I, pp. 179-181.

# CHAPTER 5

# God's Purpose Through History

(Isaiah 24-27)

1. *The Coming Judgment* (24:1-23)
2. *The Triumph of Yahweh* (25:1-12)
3. *The Hope of the Resurrection* (26:1-19)
4. *The Destruction of the Oppressor and the Restoration of the Oppressed* (26:20—27:13)

That these chapters are a unit practically every Old Testament scholar will agree. They provide an informative lesson in God's purpose through history. The advanced ideas expressed here have caused many to deny these chapters to Isaiah. Yet, there have been those equally insistent that the prophet wrote them. Some have suggested that they may have been written by the prophet as he reflected upon the world situation unfolding before him and revealed to him, but that they were never actually spoken. There seems to be some basis for this claim because the material does reflect a studied development. It deals with the great lessons which the prophet saw in the events which had taken place as well as those yet to come to pass.

Isaiah declared that judgment will come upon Israel as well as the other nations of earth because of the evil deeds of men. Yet Yahweh's purpose for them will not fail on account of their deeds, because He forgives sin and guarantees the future by the resurrection. Those who had oppressed Yahweh's people will be completely destroyed, never to rise again. Those who belonged to Yahweh, and whose sins had been forgiven, will be restored to the worship and praise after having been purged by the exile. Those in the exile will turn to Him in faith and also be restored to a position of greater glory than they had known in the past. This pattern is the Biblical pattern. If history has taught one lesson, it is that Yahweh judges sin, forgives iniquity, and restores those who turn to Him. This process is the guarantee of His purpose. The inescapable lesson of history is that the purpose of Yahweh for the world and for those who turn to Him is indestructible.

1. *The Coming Judgment* (24:1-23). The sovereign God of the universe is also its righteous judge. His judgment is impartial and complete. Verse 1 states that Yahweh is about to empty the whole earth as a result of the conditions found upon it (cf. 24:3). None will be spared, no matter what their social status or resources. Judgment will fall upon the priest as well as the people, upon the master and mistress as well as the servant, upon the buyer as well as the seller, and upon the creditor as well as the debtor (24:2). There will not be one person or group spared on the basis of rank or station (24:4). The judgment will be impartial and all-inclusive.

The basis for judgment is sin. The inhabitants of earth have transgressed the law, that is, they have revolted against Yahweh. They have passed by, disregarded His statutes. They have "broken the everlasting covenant" — the covenant made with Noah (Genesis 9:16) — which made man responsible for the basic laws of morality (24:5). As a consequence the earth and most of her inhabitants will be consumed by the wrath of Yahweh. But a small population will be spared (24:6).

The small population spared will be a joyless group. All festiveness will be gone (24:7-9). The cities will be destroyed and those people surviving will dwell behind barred doors fearing for their security (24:10). Nothing will be left except desolation (24:12) and a population as small in number as the handful of olives remaining after the tree had been shaken at harvest time, or as the few bunches of grapes overlooked in the vintage gathering (24:13).

Yet, those surviving will eventually "lift up their voice [and] shout" with joy as they praise the name of Yahweh (24:14, 15). From the west ("from the sea") they will shout His praises and the people in the west will call upon those in the east to join in the chorus. Then the coastlands ("isles of the sea") will join in the swell of praise and the "uttermost part" of the earth will follow their example (24:16). But even then all will not be well. There will first have to be a thorough purging of sin (24:20). That this had not already come to pass may be seen in the fact that the treacherous were still practicing their evil (24:16); and the guilt of transgression still rested upon the inhabitants of earth (24:20). Because of that, judgment will fall upon them; pits and snares will be placed in their routes of flight. There will be floods, and earthquakes will cause the land to come down upon the transgressors (24:17, 18). The earth will be shattered in pieces and "stagger like a drunken man, and . . . sway to and fro like a hammock; . . ." (24:20).

Following this general description of the nature of the judgment, the prophet applied it specifically. He revealed how the judgment will affect the earth's rulers and celestial beings (24:21, 22). They will be gathered together in a safe place to await their final destruction.

After all receive their due, Yahweh will ascend His throne in Jerusalem and will reign there in a glory which will cause the sun and moon to pale into insignificance (24:23).

2. *The Triumph of Yahweh* (25:1-12). Yahweh will have won a great victory when He overthrows His enemies and causes all men to fear Him (25:2, 3). When that day arrives, the redeemed will break forth in a psalm of thanksgiving (25:1-5). In this psalm Yahweh will be exalted and praised for the wonderful things which He had planned and purposed for the faithful for such a long time (25:1). Those hostile to the kingdom of God, sung of as a city, will be left in ruined heaps never to be rebuilt (25:2). Then even the enemies of Yahweh will both glorify Him and fear Him (25:3).

Israel, on the other hand, will find Yahweh "a refuge from the storm, a shade from the heat, . . ." (25:4). He will shield her and keep her citizens from all harm at the hands of their enemies (25:5).

After the digression of the psalm of thanksgiving, the narrative returns to the main theme which is the reign of Yahweh in Mount Zion (24:23, 25:6-8).

The inauguration of Yahweh in Zion will be followed by a great banquet, at which the choicest food and the finest wine will be served (25:6), and all peoples will be invited to attend. Yahweh will remove the "covering . . . and the veil," of sorrow and mourning of those who attend (25:7). The veils will come off because neither reproach nor death exist any longer (25:8). Yahweh will now be recognized as the Lord of the whole earth. Men will acknowledge and respect Him and rejoice in the salvation which He proffers (25:9).

The final paragraph of chapter 25 contrasts the conditions of those who have been up to Zion and those who populate Moab. The reason for such harsh judgment on Moab is not known. It must have been of unspeakable shame for Moab to receive such severe judgment because the people will be crushed and thrown as straw into the refuse pit (25:10, 11). Their pride will be brought low by the destruction they sustain (25:12), while Zion will be protected and safe under Yahweh's hand (25:10). What a contrast between the security of those belonging to the kingdom of God and those who are its enemies!

Yahweh and His purpose will triumph. Those who were His enemies will be destroyed.

3. *The Hope of the Resurrection* (26:1-19). "In that day" picks up the theme of 25:6-9, the feast of joy. It will be a day marked by songs of praise sung by those permitted to reside in the security and peace of Jerusalem. They will dwell in a strong city with salvation "for walls and bulwarks" (26:1). The meaning of this verse raises questions. Some see it as a reference to the fact that the city will be "saved" by her walls and bulwarks. Others suggest that the passage refers to a new condition for Jerusalem in which she no longer needs walls and bulwarks, because "in that day" Jehovah will provide her with supernatural defenses superior to any which man might erect. It may have been that the prophet had both man-made walls and supernatural defenses in mind.

The city, so formidably secured, would open her gates for the righteous to enter in (26:2). Those entering and maintaining a positive attitude toward Yahweh will know peace in its highest sense (26:3). It will be a peace based upon the strength and indestructibility of "the rock of ages" (26:4). Destruction of Yahweh's enemies will be proof of the security associated with the rock (26:5, 6).

The next division (verses 8-10) returns to the circumstances of Isaiah's own time and consists of the reflections of the prophet. The nation was still waiting for the victories promised in the righteous judgments of Yahweh (26:8, 9a), and the prophet was declaring his faith in the results of His judgments. Isaiah believed that through them the world will learn the meaning of true righteousness (26:9b, 10). It was not something the wicked will learn by being treated with favor. It was something they learn only through judgment.

After having reflected upon the conditions of his own world, the prophet prayed (11-15). He began with a petition for the overthrow of Yahweh's enemies (26:11) and the establishment of Israel in peace (26:12a). This had been Yahweh's method in the past (26:12b); it offered promise for the future (26:14, 15).

Even though promise was reflected in past events, there were some of those past events in which the people of the nation had learned little. Although they had learned the effectiveness of prayer in time of trouble (26:16), they had not learned that God was using *suffering* to turn them to Him for help (26:17, 18).

Such a despondent account seems to guarantee little hope for the future. But verse 19 changes the mood. God will cover the dead with a heavenly dew, and they will be raised to life just as a plant is raised up when a fresh supply of dew reaches its roots (26:19). In that day, the earth will cast forth the dead and they will know life again.

Most scholars agree that this is a reference to the resurrection and affirm that it is an allusion to the resurrection of the righteous. Although the nation had not learned the lessons of history and had not responded to Yahweh's chastening, there was promise for the future. It was the promise of the resurrection. Not even death can thwart Yahweh's plans for His kingdom.

4. *The Destruction of the Oppressor and the Restoration of the Oppressed* (26:20—27:13). After the remarkable interruption concerning Yahweh's triumph and the resurrection, 26:20 takes up again the idea found in 25:8 — removal of the reproach of His people.

Verses 20 and 21 warn the citizens of the kingdom to shut themselves up and await the destruction of Yahweh's enemies. Yahweh will come forth from His place and the earth will become His ally by revealing the spilled blood of the innocent which it had concealed for so long. With His strong sword He will move against the world powers who had spilled the blood (symbolized by three monsters) and He will subdue them (27:1).

Verses 2-6 are another interruption in the idea of judgment for the oppressor. They portray Yahweh's continued delight in His vineyard and reveal His commitment to its everlasting security and protection.

After the digression of 17:2-6, there follows a difficult paragraph (verses 7-11) which deals with the significance of all of Israel's afflictions. Despite the fact that Israel will suffer at the hands of Yahweh, her affliction will not be so severe as that of the other nations because of His great mercy (27:7). Through Yahweh's mercy Israel will be forgiven. She will know this forgiveness when she forsakes her evil practices (27:9). Isaiah repeated the warning that the city of the enemy will be completely destroyed and forsaken (27:10). There the cattle will feed upon the branches of the trees and the limbs will be gathered for firewood (27:11).

This section dealing with the lesson of history closes with two oracles revealing events to take place "in that day." Yahweh will separate His own from their enemies as the thresher threshes his wheat (27:12). At the sound of the trumpet those who had been threshed will come from Assyria and Egypt "to worship Jehovah in the holy mountain at Jerusalem" (27:13).

## For Further Study or Discussion

1. Does God still judge nations? What is the relationship between the character of a nation and its future?

2. Does God's purpose depend ultimately upon what any generation may do? If not, why not? If so, how do you relate it to the sovereignty of God?

3. What role does faith have in the life of a nation? Do you believe it provides security for a nation? In what way? How do you explain the difficulties of some so-called nations of faith?

4. What lessons from history may be learned about God and nations? Is God's purpose in history to be realized? How?

5. What is unique about a covenantal relationship? Read the article on "Covenant" in IDB, Volume I, pp. 714-723.

6. Read the article on "Resurrection" in IDB, Volume IV, pp. 39-43 and in ZPBD, pp. 713, 714.

# CHAPTER 6

# Men and Flesh
# or God and Spirit

### (Isaiah 28-33)

Most of the material in this section is assigned to the period immediately before and leading up to 701 B.C. One of the primary themes of these chapters is the prophet's denunciation of the treaty between Egypt and Judah, in which they mutually agree to revolt against Assyria. A second emphasis is upon the contrasts between present and future conditions.

1. *A Covenant with Death* (28:1-29). With chapter 28, Isaiah opened his volume dealing with the revolt against Sennacherib. He began by quoting a prophecy which had been announced concerning Samaria before her fall in 722 B.C. This may have been for effect. Since the event may have been remembered and since some may even have remembered the very prophecy, Isaiah was seeking to impress upon his hearers the importance of what he was about to say.

(a) THE FALL OF SAMARIA (28:1-6). Samaria was a beautiful walled city upon the brow of a hill set in the center of a beautiful valley (I Kings 16:24); but because of the conditions in the city, the walls had become like a wilted wreath of flowers (28:1). This was brought on by drunkenness and its attendant evils. Because of these prevailing conditions Yahweh planned to direct "a mighty and strong one" (the Assyrians) against Samaria and then would flood (overrun) the city with such force that it would be flattened. The destruction was compared to the anxious consumption of the first ripe fig of the season by the cultivator of the orchard (28:3, 4). In sharp contrast there follows a sentence pointing to the glories of the Messianic Age (28:5, 6). "In that day" there will be a crown also, but not one of pride. It will be a symbol of divine favor upon "the residue of his people" (the remnant). This vital relationship between Yahweh and the remnant will cause justice to be administered and the defenders of their dwelling place to "turn back the battle at the gate." The defenders will be powerful enough to secure the peace of those dwelling in the city.

(b) The Folly of Trusting in Egypt (28:7-22). The conditions in Judah at the time (705-701 B.C.) were similiar to those in Samaria earlier (28:7, 8), and it was implied that Judah could expect similar consequences. The intemperate leaders, civil and spiritual, were unable to bear their responsibilities effectively (28:7b). The prophets "err in vision," that is, misinterpreted their visions; and the priests "stumble in judgment," that is, they were unable to interpret the law effectively in religious matters.

Isaiah may have made this prediction at a festive occasion during which the leaders celebrated their decision to renounce their loyalty to Assyria. The leaders, confronted by Isaiah, accused him in turn. He was belittling them, they said, as if he were a teacher scolding a young pupil (28:9, 10). Though the contents of verses 9 and 10 are difficult to interpret, it seems that they contain the responses of the various groups to the counsel of Isaiah. The first question, "Whom will he teach knowledge?" may have expressed the reaction of the priests. The second question, "Whom will he make to understand the message?" may have reflected the response of the prophets. The third question, "Them that are weaned . . . ?" may have revealed the attitude of the nobles. Then, as though they were mocking the prophet, they recited in brief phrases the rules for teaching children. Yet, Isaiah was not to be outdone by them. He told them that Yahweh was about to take men of another tongue to speak to them (28:11). Since they had refused the instructions of Isaiah, they would be given other teachers — the Assyrians. That enemy could deliver as devastating a blow with words as they did with swords.

Following this, Isaiah elaborated upon the folly of the policy and behavior of the nation. The leaders had turned the nation toward false gods and toward practices not permitted by the law. They claimed "a covenant with death," which may have been a reference, as some suggest, to the claim that they had agreed to serve the gods of the underworld if the gods in turn would protect them (28:15). In any case, Isaiah condemned them for their action and accused them of making lies and falsehoods (false gods) their refuge. He stated that there was but one secure foundation on which to build, and that was faith in the plan and purpose of Yahweh (28:16). That cornerstone was not Yahweh Himself because it was He who had set it in the first place. Though it contained meaning for those who heard Isaiah preach, it also was an allusion to the Messiah in whom Yahweh realized His purpose (Romans 9:33; 10:11; and I Peter 2:6-8).

There were standards for building upon the foundation which Yahweh had laid; they were justice and righteousness (28:17a). In fact, they were the equivalent of a plumb and plumb line in a physical structure. Every structure not built by these standards would fail to provide deliverance and security (28:17b). When the judgment (the Assyrians) passed through, the people's misplaced faith would fail them completely (28:18). The destruction would persist until it fell upon every conspirator (28:19). In that day all words from the prophet would be so negative that he would draw back from his responsibility to speak (28:19b).

Such conditions were to prevail because the objects of their faith and plans for their future were inadequate. They were as inadequate, comparatively speaking, as a bed too short to lie upon or a blanket too narrow to cover one (28:20). In light of these circumstances there was going to be nothing to keep Yahweh from doing "his strange work." In this case, it would be His use of the Assyrians to fight against His own people (28:21). He would repeat what He had done to the Philistines, only this time it would be upon His own people (see II Samuel 5:20, 25).

Verse 22 contains a concluding warning in which the prophet told the scoffer to cease his laughter lest he be so firmly bound that there would be no way of escape. By implication Isaiah was saying, "cease scoffing and you will be delivered from destruction." Even so, it appears that the prophet did not have much hope that the tragedy could be averted.

(c) A PARABLE FROM THE FARM (28:23-29). After an introduction to the parable (28:23), there follows a section dealing with the matter of plowing and sowing (28:24-26). The farmer plows with the purpose of sowing in mind. He does not year in and year out only break up the ground and harrow it (28:24), he plows and harrows that he may plant the crop. When the land is properly prepared then the husbandman plants his seed. He scatters the fitches and sows the cummin (both plants used as seasonings); but he plants the wheat and barley in rows and plants around them a protective hedge (28:25).

As it was with the farmer, so was it with Yahweh. The purpose of Yahweh's plowing (judgment) was the same as that of the farmer. That is, there was a purpose beyond the judgment of Yahweh. That purpose would be realized through the seed which would be sown.

After plowing and sowing there follows the figure of threshing (28:27-29). Threshing is here synonymous with Yahweh's judgment. Threshing too serves its purpose. Yet all crops are not gathered the same way (28:27, 28). The fitches are not reaped with the same tools used to reap other grain; nor is the cummin threshed by driving a cart wheel over it, since that would ruin it. So, as the farmer uses a particular method to harvest a particular grain, Yahweh would use a special method to harvest the seed of Judah, a nucleus or a remnant of the true Israel. The prophet is saying that Yahweh's judgment is carefully and purposefully planned. As after plowing there would be sowing and after threshing there is seed, so, after the judgment there would be a people of Yahweh.

2. *Jerusalem Humiliated and Delivered* (29:1-24). In somewhat the same manner in which he opened chapter 28 — with a reference to judgment upon Samaria — the prophet opens this chapter. He announces a threat to Jerusalem.

(a) JERUSALEM AFFLICTED AND DELIVERED (29:1-8). Instead of "Jerusalem" the text has "Ariel." Various explanations of this usage have been made. One explanation is that it means "lion of God." This, however, seems unlikely because in such a case Jerusalem would be depicted in a favorable light rather than the obviously unfavorable one implied in the context. Another explanation is that it means "hearth of God." This reading seems preferable in light of verse 2, which speaks of Jerusalem as a place for the flames of war, a hearth unto Yahweh. According to this explanation, Jerusalem was going to be an "altar" upon which the flames of war would burn (cf. 29:6).

The chapter began with Jerusalem in a festive mood (29:1). It may actually have been the time of the Feast of Tabernacles that the words were delivered. The prophet said, ". . . let the feast come round . . ." By doing so he may have been suggesting their cessation; some have contended that implicit in these words was the suggestion that they would "come round" only a limited number of times. This would have been a fitting introduction to the following verses which announce an attack on Jerusalem. Verse 1 began with "ho" which is to be translated "woe." Thus the section (29:1-4) was a lament over the potential destruction which the city would experience. It would be a siege like David's siege (29:3; cf. II Samuel 5:6, 7). This translation of verse 3 is supported by the Septuagint and seems to be a better one than "I will encamp against thee round about."

As a result of the siege, the city would be prostrate in the dust and from her prostrate position she would mourn and lament (29: 4, cf. 29:2).

Verses 5 and 6, without any forewarning, reversed the picture. Just as the enemy was about to lay hold upon the city, Yahweh would suddenly rout them (the Assyrians) and the city would be saved. Then, as though awakened from a nightmare, the city would find that she had been spared and that the enemy had been left desolate (29:7, 8).

(b) THE CAUSES OF THE AFFLICTIONS OF YAHWEH (29:9-16). Taking up again the message in verses 1-4, Isaiah predicts that the people will "be amazed" (stupefied) and "blinded" to the point that they will stagger about like drunkards in the confusion brought about by their practices (29:9, 10). Because of their sins Yahweh has sent deep sleep upon them. He has so closed their eyes and muffled their ears that they have lost all ability to interpret His purpose (29:10-13).

But this is not all that the prophet reveals. He declares that their religion is superficial and vain. The people were dutiful in practicing religion but it was the religion of words and not of the heart. Their "reverence" for Yahweh was in reality only obedience to man's instruction. There was no true reverence in their lives (29:13). Yet Yahweh was not ready to cast His people aside. He planned to do marvelous things with them again (29:14). He was going to bring about a recurrence of true religious dedication and devotion, a religion of reality and not one of pretense. It was to be based upon an understanding superior to that of their wise men —

an understanding which could come only after their own wisdom had been proven false (29:14).

Verses 15 and 16 announce a reproach upon those who refused the true wisdom of Yahweh and claimed they were following His direction when they were not. They tried to conceal their true character and intent, but the prophet was able to unmask their folly. He accused them of turning things upside down. They had, by their actions, denied Yahweh a voice in the formulation of their plans. This was an effrontery which was appalling. It was as unreasonable as declaring that there was no difference between the clay and the potter (29:16). They could no more conceal their plans from Yahweh than they could expect those plans to succeed without His instruction.

(c) A GLANCE AT THE FUTURE (29:17-24). In two brief sections (verses 17-21 and 22-24) the prophet glances into the future. Beyond the tragic picture just described there was coming a day in which the remnant will be restored and secured. The earth will be renewed and those who had been deaf and blind to the purposes of Yahweh will see and hear (29:18). The "meek" (oppressed) and "poor," who had known little to rejoice over in the past, will know the joy of Yahweh's deliverance (29:19). This deliverance will result in His destruction of their oppressors and dispensers of injustice (29:20, 21). When that day dawns the house of Jacob, rather than being ashamed and pale with fear, will reverence Yahweh and place itself in subjection to Him (29:22-24).

3. *Planning Without God* (30, 31). Chapter 30 takes up and develops the theme of the rebellion against Assyria. Isaiah reveals that their secret dealings (29:15), now known to him, are not rebellion against Assyria — they are in reality rebellion against Yahweh, because they are contrary to His will.

(a) THE JUDEAN EMBASSY (30:1-7). Judah seized upon the occasion of the death of Sargon (705 B.C.) as the opportune time to rebel against kingless Assyria. She reached the decision without taking counsel with Yahweh and made a treaty with Egypt not in keeping with His will. She was, through the treaty, adding another sin to the sin of concealing her purpose and going against the will of Yahweh (30:1). They had not asked anything of Him but had instead fled to the "strength of Pharaoh . . . to take refuge in the shadow of Egypt!" (30:2). Isaiah knew she had chosen a disastrous course.

The plans which Judah had made were in themselves foolish (30:3-5). Even though the Egyptians had reached the extreme limits of Lower Egypt (Zoan and Hames), they were not strong enough to vanquish the Assyrians. They would be easily defeated and would through their defeat bring shame upon their allies (30:5).

Verses 6 and 7 refer to the caravans traversing the desert between Judah and Egypt. Sending these gift-laden emissaries to Egypt were of no avail, because Judah was putting her hope in "a people that shall not profit" her. "For Egypt helpeth in vain, and to no purpose . . ." because proud Rahab (the sea monster which had become a symbol for Egypt) "sitteth still" and is unable to deliver Judah (30:7).

(b) THE RELATIONSHIP BETWEEN FAITH AND CIRCUMSTANCE (30:8-26). The people, as a result of their lack of faith, rejected the words of the true prophet for those of the false prophet. This could lead only to insecurity and helplessness. To know the security and strength they longed for required faith in Yahweh.

In verse 8 Isaiah was told to write down his messages on the folly of reliance upon Egypt. (Some have suggested that these may have been the substance of chapters 28-32.) The reason for recording these words was that they might be "for a witness forever" (cf. 8:16-18).

The words written were in protest against the faithlessness of Judah (30:9-11). Judah was made up of a rebellious people who would not receive the teaching of Yahweh (30:9). They sought to silence the true prophets. They wanted to be deceived by the "smooth things," concepts with which they agreed but which were, nevertheless, untrue (30:10). In doing so they had demanded a cessation of all true revelation from Yahweh (30:11).

In response to their conduct, Yahweh revealed that the warnings delivered against reliance upon Egypt ("this word") were but a limited condemnation. They would as a result of their policy suffer greater disaster (30:12-14). But on the other hand, the people of Judah were told how they might expect to avert that disaster: "In returning" to Yahweh and in surrendering ("rest") they shall be saved (as the people of Yahweh). With salvation comes a calm ("quietness") dependence on Yahweh which would give them the courage (strength) to do His will (30:15). Judah would not, however, respond to Yahweh's invitation (30:15b).

Verse 16 describes the defeat of those who seek to escape the consequences of their folly but who are overtaken by an enemy of greater swiftness. One of that enemy was going to rout a thousand, and in the end all that remained would be as "a beacon" (flagstaff) left behind by a fleeing army (30:17).

After these severe words, Isaiah returned (30:18-26) to his sincere belief that, in spite of all of Judah's folly, Yahweh would realize His purpose for the "chosen nation." These words of assurance needed to be shared with the people. So Isaiah stated that Yahweh was waiting hopefully and expectantly for the moment of the change in their state (30:18). One condition for the change is their sincere prayer to Yahweh (30:19). When they seek Him, He will hear their prayers and they will again hear His word (30:21). Their teachers (the prophets) will teach again (30:20) and Jehovah will not remain hidden or silent. They will listen to the prophets and forsake their idols (30:22). There will be a better day and it will come through the work of Yahweh.

Along with the spiritual blessings to be experienced, there will be attendant material blessings (30:23-26). The rain will be sufficient to guarantee abundant crops and feed for the animals (30:23, 24). Even the barren areas will have sources of water while the enemies of Yahweh suffer destruction at His hands (30:25). At that time, the light of an entire week will be crowded into one day (30:26). There will be enough time provided for all these wonders to be accomplished.

By dealing with the conditions which brought on affliction and disclosing the possibilities for those who turn to Yahweh in faith, Isaiah was revealing the relationship between faith and circumstance. Faithlessness brings compromise and compromise brings judgment. Faith brings mercy and mercy blessings, both spiritual and material.

(c) YAHWEH'S HANDLING OF THE ASSYRIANS (30:27-33). These verses contain the vision of the destruction of the Assyrians. They were to be destroyed through the power and wrath of Yahweh (30:27, 28). The "name of Jehovah" is a reference to a demonstration of His presence in the storm. The demonstration was for the purpose of sifting (destroying) the enemy and turning him away from his goal as one would turn an animal with a bridle.

In the meantime there was going to be rejoicing by the Israelites, rejoicing like that of the Passover. Isaiah was saying that they were to have, as a consequence of the destruction of the Assyrians, an occasion like the Passover to celebrate (30:29).

Yahweh's voice, the manifestation of His power, will smite the enemy with a devastating blow (30:30, 32). He had, in fact, pre-prepared for them a sacrificial fire (a tophet) stoked by the fire of His breath (30:33). The Assyrians had no hope of survival; therefore, the people of Yahweh had occasion to rejoice.

(d) THE FOLLY OF TRUSTING IN EGYPT (31:1-3). With every indication that the negotiations with Egypt had been concluded, Isaiah turned his attention to the folly of this action. Judah had turned her back upon Yahweh for the futile help of men (31:1-3). She was condemned for putting her faith in the strength of Egypt's horses and chariots. To Isaiah this was a breach of faith. It was folly to trust in Egypt rather than the "Holy One of Israel." Though Judah must have congratulated herself over the wisdom displayed in the accomplishment of the treaty, Isaiah reminded her that Yahweh too was wise. He had a purpose and was powerful enough to bring it to fruition. He can bring evil upon the one who turned away to place her faith in Egypt rather than Himself, and He would at the same time judge her helper (Egypt) (31:2).

The reason for the prophet's severe words is to be found in his understanding of the moral government of the universe. Yahweh was in control of history, and His purpose could not be undone by any or all those opposing Him. His people could count on Him for victory. They did not need to scheme or plot with the nations of earth in the hopes of guarantying their future. Isaiah was simply stating in 31:3 that to turn to Egypt was to turn to man and therein to lack a confident trust in Yahweh.

(e) YAHWEH WILL SAVE JERUSALEM WITHOUT HELP (31:4-9). And yet Yahweh does not leave the inhabitants without hope. He declares that He will defend Jerusalem against the enemy. He will not be dismayed by the size of the Assyrian army (31:4). He will protect Jerusalem as birds hovering over their nests protect their young (31:5), but Jerusalem must turn to Him and cast aside all substitutes (31:6, 7). This will guarantee the fall of Assyria, not by the might of man, but by the power of Jehovah (31:8, 9).

4. *The Reign of One in Righteousness* (32:1-20). Judah had made a tragic mistake in turning to Egypt, but there would be a time that she would be secure in a society created and sustained by One who would occupy David's throne and reign in righteousness.

(a) THE PICTURE OF A TRANSFORMED SOCIETY (32:1-8). A

transformed society is one in which Yahweh's principles of righteousness and justice will be practiced. In due time, according to Isaiah, such conditions will exist. There will be a king (the ruler on David's throne) whose righteous reign will be the standard for the princes, who will then reign in justice as the king reigned in righteousness (32:1). The leaders ("a man") will be protectors ("covet" and "shade") of the inhabitants rather than exploiters (32:2).

In that day, the ruler will see the need and hear the cry of the populace (32:3). Then the impatient will have understanding and exercise good judgment, while the stammerer will speak easily and plainly (32:4). Ungodly men will no longer be looked upon as nobles and princes (32:5). They will be recognized for what they are — evil, wicked, foolish men (32:6, 7). The noble will be the generous who will by work establish his nobility (32:8).

(b) THE THREAT TO THE WOMEN OF JERUSALEM (32:9-20). The women of Jerusalem had shown little if any concern for the conditions which had been so criticized by the prophet. They were concerned only with themselves. Isaiah sought to awaken them to reality by announcing a forthcoming disaster (32:9, 10). So certain was he of its accomplishment that he called upon them to put on sackcloth and beat upon their breasts in anguish (32:11-14). Yet, even this was not to be considered the end, because after the purging there will be a new world. Through the Spirit of Yahweh there will be a renewal of nature (32:15) and a rebirth of righteousness (32:16), and out of these will be established a society of peace and security (32:17, 18). In the meantime, judgment was coming (32:19); but after it has passed, there will be a time of plenty (32:20). The peasant will sow without the dread of failure and his animals will find provender everywhere.

In this chapter, as in many other sections, Isaiah moved back and forth between the conditions which deserved the judgment of Yahweh and the hope of the future after the purging. This was a useful device which pronounced the end for those who were the enemies of Yahweh, and which at the same time gave words of promise to those who belonged to Him or those who would turn to Him in repentance. Despite all which might suggest otherwise, there is to be a future for the faithful; and there will always be those who remain faithful and trust in the righteousness of Yahweh. Beyond the present "veil of tears" there will be a new world and a new king and a new people of God.

5. *A Quiet Habitation* (33:1-24). After a statement of condemnation and retribution on an unidentified foe — believed by some to have been the Assyrians (33:1) — Isaiah, or the people, entreated Yahweh to be the arm of His people in their time of need (33:2). Because of their hope, the nation awaited the speedy overthrow of the enemy and the acquisition of the spoils of its lands (33:3, 4). After that, Zion was going to be filled with justice and righteousness (33:5, 6). At the present there was oppression, waste, contempt, and desolation (33:7-9), but all was not lost because the prophet heard Yahweh declare an end to the invader (33:10-13). The enemy was to be totally ravaged by the wrath of Yahweh and Israel's future would be guaranteed.

Verses 14-16 contrast the effects of Yahweh's presence upon the unrighteous (33:14) and upon the righteous (33:15, 16).

One day, in the age to come, the righteous will see the Messianic King ruling over His vast domain and will find it next to impossible to recall the conditions under which they were now living (33:17-19). The new Jerusalem will, through Yahweh's own protection, become a quiet habitation (33:20, 21). There the people will know an abiding peace. Yahweh will be both their ruler and deliverer. There will be no sickness (a sign that one was suffering the displeasure of Yahweh) because of unconfessed sin, for in that day sin will be forgiven and guilt will be expiated (33:24).

## FOR FURTHER STUDY OR DISCUSSION

1. Read article on "Sennacherib" in IDB, Volume IV, pp. 270-272 and in ZPBD, pp. 769, 770.

2. Read article on "Samaria" in ZPBD, p. 744 and in IDB, Volume IV, pp. 182-188.

3. If reliance upon nations in Isaiah's day was wrong, what about it now? How do nations justify their alliances with each other? How do you explain it?

4. Was Isaiah saying Jerusalem would remain inviolable regardless of her character?

5. Did the deliverance of Jerusalem mean she would remain delivered for all time thereafter?

6. What conditions brought on the afflictions of 29:9-16? Do any of these exist today? What do they imply?

7. Do nations consider God in their planning today? Which ones? Are plans without God limited? What do you feel results from nations seeking God's direction in their planning?

8. Is there a relationship between faith and circumstance? Give a personal example. Give an international example.

9. What is your idea of a transformed society? Can you give a modern example? If so, why? If not, why not?

CHAPTER 7

# A Day of Vengeance,
# a Year of Recompense

(Isaiah 34, 35)

In chapters 34 and 35 Isaiah continues his practice of contrasting judgment with deliverance. The contrast here is between the judgment of the nations, Edom in particular, and the glory associated with the restoration of Israel.

1. *Judgment Upon the Nations* (34:1-4). The enemies of the people of Yahweh were summoned to draw near and hear the announcement of their destruction (34:1, cf. Micah 1:2). It was to be a judgment which included the earth and "all things that come forth of it." It was to be an all-inclusive judgment. The nations, because of their enmity toward Zion, are doomed to complete destruction. Just as an animal was utterly consumed when placed as a sacrifice upon the altar, so these nations will be utterly consumed when they are placed as a sacrifice upon the altar of Yahweh's judgment.

Verse 3 described the scene of the destruction. The dead pollute the atmosphere with their decomposing bodies, either because there were too many to bury or because there were too few survivors to bury them. It might have been that the dead were left unburied only as an expression of contempt. The flow of their blood melts the mountains and dissolves the hills. The whole earth is involved in the destruction which Yahweh planned for His enemies.

The judgment upon the nations involves not only the earth — the heavens also will be affected. The sky, envisioned as a scroll, will "be rolled together . . ." as a sheet of parchment which was no

longer being held open by the hand of the reader. The stars
and planets will fade away and fall as the leaves on the vine or
fig tree (34:4). Both heaven and earth will be altered when the
judgment of Yahweh falls upon the nations. And the change will be
sudden and total.

2. *Judgment Upon Edom* (34:5-17). As though Edom had been
singled out to represent the enemies of Yahweh and His people, the
emphasis in this chapter is on the slaughter of the Edomites. The
sword of Yahweh will drink its fill of wrath in heaven as a part of
its preparation for the task assigned it on earth, judgment upon
Edom (34:5). The Edomites, who had been declared a people
consecrated to Yahweh, were compared to the various sacrificial animals. As these animals were offered in sacrifice, so would the
Edomites be offered in Bozrah and all across the face of the nation
(34:6, 7). It will be "a day of vengeance" upon those who were
guilty of being the enemies of Yahweh and His people as well as
"a year of recompense," of revenge, in the cause of Zion (34:8).
The references to "day" and "year" are to indefinite periods of time.

After the announcement that Edom was to be dealt with so
severely, there follows a description of the conflagration and desolation which result from the consuming power of Yahweh's wrath. The
images used to describe the condition are comparable to those used
to describe the overthrow of Sodom and Gomorrah (34:9, cf.
Genesis 19:24-28). The land will burn day and night as though it
were pitch. The smoke from the conflagration will rise generation
after generation, suggesting that Edom would remain a perpetual
wasteland which all men would seek to avoid on their journeys
(34:10). The sole occupants of the land will be wild animals and
birds (34:11a). Where men once lived there will be nothing. The
inhabitants will be lost and their dwellings overgrown with nettles
and brambles (34:12-15).

Verse 16 is an admonition for future generations to seek out
"the book of Jehovah," which contained the pronouncements upon
Edom, to see if these declarations had not come to pass. Not one of
these pronouncements will "want her mate" (her companion); each
will have been fulfilled. Just as conquerors divide the land by lot,
so will Edom be apportioned among the wild beasts. And the land
will remain a habitation for wild creatures "from generation to generation (34:17).

3. *The Future Blessedness of the Ransomed of Yahweh* (35:

1-10). Chapter 35, in sharp contrast to chapter 34, presents two conditions which would bring about the future blessedness of the redeemed: Verses 1-6 show the great change which wrought by Yahweh upon the desolate places and in the circumstances of the redeemed; verses 7-10 elaborate upon His purpose for those who had been so long afflicted and denied their homeland.

In that day, the desolate places will rejoice over their transformed state (35:1-2). This may have been a reference to the desolation left as a result of the destruction of Judah, or it may have been a reference to the desert which lay between the exiles and their homeland. In either case, the desolate areas will burst forth with blossoms and singing (35:1, 2). Lebanon, Carmel, and Sharon once more will be given the beauty for which they had been traditionally known. Nature will undergo a complete change, and even the most barren areas will be clothed in beauty.

Nature, however, is not the only recipient of Yahweh's transforming power. The despondent, weakened, and fearful will be healed and strengthened by Him (35:3-6). Those who had been taken captive, those with weak hands (hanging at their sides in resignation to their fate), those with feeble and tottering knees (tottering because the people had been driven so hard by their captors), and those who were afraid — all would be told to look to Yahweh (35:3-4). He would come with vengeance (retribution) for their captors and with recompense (deliverance) for His own.

When at last Yahweh takes up the cause of His captive people even the most seriously incapacitated will be healed: the blind, the deaf, the lame, and the dumb will be free from their infirmities (35:5-6). Every disability will be removed; and, as those who had been restored made their way up to Zion, they will find the deserts themselves blessed with streams of water. Because of these blessings, all those who formerly had been beset by handicaps and limitations will break forth with singing (35:6). It will be a time in which Yahweh meets every need so that the recipients of His salvation might be enabled to return to the Promised Land.

Verses 8-10 continue the account of the preparation for the return of the redeemed and describe the highway which Yahweh is making ready for them. This highway would be called "Holiness," so named because it would lead back to the Holy Place in Jerusalem. The unclean would not be allowed upon it. It will be for the redeemed, those ransomed from the nations in which they had lived since the captivity (35:8). This highway will be such an obvious way and such a secure way that the simplest will not be led astray from it, nor will the traveler need to fear the threat of wild beasts as he journeyed homeward through the wilderness. Every danger will be removed (35:9).

With the way established and secured, "the ransomed of Jehovah shall return, and come with singing unto Zion" (35:10). The exiles will make their way back to Zion singing and rejoicing, and even their "heads" (countenances) will show their joy. In that day, "all sorrow and sighing" will be banished. Yahweh's people will have reached the Promised Land and there they will no longer know suffering and privation.

### FOR FURTHER STUDY OR DISCUSSION

1. Read article on "Edom" in IDB, Volume II, pp. 24-26.
2. Does Edom seem to represent all that was evil in Isaiah's day? Have there appeared to be other such nations in history? Name some. What has happened to them?
3. Does the Bible always promise a better day for the people of Jehovah? Do you believe this? Do most people? How do you explain those who do not.
4. Does God still control nature? Does it still respond to Jehovah's purpose? What has caused some to doubt this?
5. May all men who believe in the goodness of God expect better things? On what conditions? Is it inevitable in this life? If so, how? If not, when?

# CHAPTER 8

# The Provocation of Prayer and the Entreaty of Tears

## (Isaiah 36-39)

Isaiah 36-39 forms a historical appendix to the first part of the book of Isaiah. The content of these chapters is practically the same as II Kings 18:13—20:19. This has posed a question concerning the relationship of the material in Isaiah to that of II Kings. In their attempts to deal with the question, some have held that chapters 36-39 were taken from the book of II Kings. Others have contended that Isaiah was the author of the material and that his words were placed in Kings by the compiler of the historical books. And there are those, who, on the basis of II Chronicles 32:32, contend that the author of this book actually had the book of Isaiah before him as a source. It has also been suggested that in addition to serving as an appendix to the first major division of the book of Isaiah, chapters 36-39 function as a bridge between Isaiah 1-35 and 40-66. Since the context of the material in Isaiah 1-35 is the Assyrian Period, and since the context of 40-66 is the Babylonian Period, it is suggested that chapters 36-39 provide the materials needed to make the transition from one era to the other. They contain references to the final Assyrian effort in Judah, a description of the first Babylonian contact, and Isaiah's prediction of the exile.

1. *The Invasion of Judah by Sennacherib* (36:1-22). In the fourteenth year of Hezekiah, Sennacherib marched against the cities

of Judah and according to the Assyrian's count captured forty-six of them (36:1). Included in the list was Lachish. While at Lachish, Sennacherib sent the Rabshakeh (the title given the chief envoy) to take possession of Jerusalem (36:2; cf. II Kings 18:17). Upon his arrival at the city, the Rabshakeh stood in the same general area in which Isaiah had confronted Ahaz over thirty years earlier (36:3; cf. 7:3). During this negotiation, Judah was represented by three civilian officials — Eliakim, Shebna and Joah (36:3).

Verses 4-10 contain the speech of the Rabshakeh. Since the small nation of Judah was attempting to pit herself against the might of Assyria, the chief envoy asked upon what she was depending for security (36:4-5). Then, displaying his knowledge of her treaty with Egypt, the Rabshakeh told the three officials that Egypt was as unreliable and detrimental as a "bruised" reed (36:6). Judah could not depend upon Egypt. But the Assyrian went even further by adding that she could not depend upon Yahweh. This startling remark of the Rabshakeh was based upon his belief that Hezekiah had committed a harmful act when he destroyed the local altars and required the people to worship at Jerusalem (36:7). The Rabshakeh felt that the king should have allowed these local altars to remain as they were. Then the Assyrian wagered (a better translation than "give pledges") that these people would not have the horsemen to mount two thousand horses if they were given to them (36:8). This was doubtless true. In fact, the Rabshakeh expressed the belief that the strength of Hezekiah was not equal to that of even a provincial governor in the Assyrian Empire, and yet he was threatening revolt (36:9). In addition to all this, the representatives of Hezekiah were told that the Assyrians had been sent by Yahweh to destroy Judah (36:10). This question immediately poses itself: Why was the Rabshakeh claiming such a role for the Assyrians? Was it because of the desecration of the sanctuaries? Was it because he had learned of Isaiah's words in 10:5, 6? Whatever the basis of his claim, it was clear that he felt the prospect for Judah was an ominous one.

Because they were fearful of the people's reaction to this claim, Hezekiah's ministers entreated the Rabshakeh to speak to them in Aramaic (the language of diplomacy) rather than in the language of the populace (36:11). He refused. He proclaimed even more loudly and more forcibly the consequences of Hezekiah's policy so that all the people might hear and make their opinions known (36:12-20).

The citizens of Jerusalem were told that Hezekiah was deceiving them by leading them to believe that the treaty with Egypt would deliver them from Assyrian domination (36:14). They were told to give up the idea that Yahweh would deliver them since their only hope was in surrender (36:15, 16). But even this would be merely a temporary deliverance because they would eventually be deported. Yet when they were taken from their homeland, it would be to a country in which they would find abundance (36:17). They were not to resist because the conditions which Assyria offered were as appealing as those found in their own land.

In verses 18-20, the Rabshakeh recounted the successes of the Assyrian armies and the failures of god after god to deliver their people from the Assyrian forces. On the basis of past occurrences he was stating that Yahweh would not be able to deliver Jerusalem (36:20).

The response of the populace to the reasoning of the Assyrian emissary was silence (36:21). Then the three Jewish representatives, with their clothing rent to reflect their great distress over the words of Rabshakeh reported to Hezekiah (36:22).

2. *Hezekiah's Response to the Rabshakeh's Threat* (37:1-7). Upon hearing the report, and after going to the Temple to pray, Hezekiah sent a committee to Isaiah for counsel. The group was composed of the "elders of the priests" along with Eliakim and Shebna (37:1, 2). They reported to Isaiah that it was a day of distress, rebuke, and rejection. It was a situation comparable to that of a pregnant woman's coming to the time of delivery without having the strength to bring forth her child (37:3). In light of the distress, Isaiah was asked to intercede in their behalf (37:4).

Isaiah's response to their entreaty was electric. It far exceeded their request (37:6-8). The prophet said: "Jehovah has already spoken to me. Do not fear the Assyrian. Our God will put a spirit of fear in the Assyrian ruler which will cause him to return to his own country, in which he will die by a sword." The cause of his fear was the approach of Tirhakah, king of Ethiopia (37:9).

3. *Assyria Threatened by Tirhakah; Sennacherib's Letter* (37:8-20). When the Rabshakeh returned to report to Sennacherib, he found him fighting against Libnah (one of the cities of Judah which he subsequently conquered) and faced with a threat from Tirhakah (37:8, 9). Because of these difficulties, and perhaps because he was

hoping to secure Jerusalem in the meanwhile, Sennacherib sent Hezekiah a letter containing much of the Rabshakeh's logic but with the added contention that the king of Judah had been deceived by Yahweh (37:10-13).

Upon receipt of this message, Hezekiah went up to the Temple. There he spread out the letter before Yahweh with the prayer that He take note of the proud boastings and defiant spirit of the Assyrians (37:14-17). The king acknowledged the accomplishments of the Assyrians, but insisted that their deities were not divine (37:18, 19). Therefore, in light of the attitude of the Assyrians and the nature of their gods, Hezekiah entreated Yahweh to demonstrate the fact that He alone was God (37:20). Yahweh's response came in the form of a message from Isaiah.

4. *Yahweh's Message to Hezekiah* (37:21-35). Yahweh's answer to Hezekiah's prayer came in the form of a taunt-song voiced by Isaiah (37:22-29). Although the ignominious defeat of the Assyrian was predicted, the song held that Jerusalem would remain ("virgin") unmolested (37:22, 23). The proud boastings of the Assyrians were belittled by the taunt (37:24, 25). They did not realize that the successes which they had known were but a fragment of Yahweh's all-inclusive purpose (37:26, 27). He had kept watch over all their actions; and because of their attitude toward Him and His people, He would return them to the place from which they had come (37:28, 29).

Following a three-year period of privation, there would dawn a new age in which all of Israel's hopes and dreams would come to pass (37:30-32).

Verses 33-35 contain an oracle concerning the future of Sennacherib. He would be unable to besiege Jerusalem, and in due time would leave by the route he initially had taken up to the city (37:33, 34). Yahweh Himself would defend Jerusalem. He would do this for the sake of His name, which Sennacherib had blasphemed. And it would also be for the sake of David, His servant, whom He had promised that there would always be one to occupy his throne (37:35).

The last paragraph in chapter 37 describes the rout and murder of Sennacherib. The angel of Yahweh smote the Assyrian host (whether by plague or pestilence is not known) and Sennacherib fled to Nineveh (37:37). Sometime later he was murdered by two of his sons, Adrammelech and Sharezer, and then succeeded by another son Esar-haddon (37:38). Thus ended a grave threat to Jerusalem.

5. *The Sickness and Recovery of Hezekiah* (38:1-22). Sometime before the arrival of the envoys sent by the king of Babylonia (*ca.* 705 B.C.), discussed in chapter 39, Hezekiah was taken ill and was told that he was going to die (38:1). He was instructed by the prophet, speaking on Yahweh's behalf, to set his house in order. Obedience to these instructions entailed his giving the necessary counsel or directions to those who would survive him (cf. II Kings 2:1-9).

In response to the words of the prophet, Hezekiah turned his face to the wall and prayed; it was as though he were turning away from all who might have been present (38:2). The ruler asked Yahweh to remember that he had walked before Him "in truth and with a perfect heart" — his heart was wholly dedicated to Him and His purpose (38:3). It was with prayers and bitter tears that Hezekiah pled with Yahweh.

Yahweh heard the prayer of the king and sent Isaiah to tell him that his life would be extended fifteen years and that the city of Jerusalem would be saved from the Assyrians (38:5, 6). As proof of Yahweh's promise the sun would be made to reverse itself, thus affecting the length of the shadow thrown upon the steps of Hezekiah's private entrance (38:7, 8; cf. II Kings 20:1-11).

Hezekiah's song of thanksgiving, which had two stanzas, constitutes the major portion of the remainder of chapter 38. The first stanza, found in verses 10-14, describes the circumstances of the king's illness. The second stanza, verses 15-20, reflects the gratitude and delight of the king upon his recovery.

Hezekiah was greatly distressed at the thought of death. To die in the noontide of his days, the midpoint of his life, would cut him off prematurely from all communion with Yahweh and leave him with those who had preceded him in death (38:10, 11). The beliefs and doctrines Hezekiah had been taught did not include the promises of heaven as they came to be revealed in due course. Therefore, he did not associate Yahweh with Sheol (the abode of the dead). He spoke of his life in terms of a shepherd's tent and a soon-finished tapestry. The tent was set up quickly and then suddenly taken down. The tapestry, when finished, was immediately cut from the loom and sold. Hezekiah saw his life being snatched away in just such a manner. Verse 13 with a slight amendation

reads, "I cried until morning" because the pain was as that suffered
by one torn and crushed by a lion. He spent the night as would a
swallow, a crane, or a dove, moaning and twittering in plaintive
sounds. His face was turned toward the dwelling place of Yahweh
in the hope that He would become "surety" for him, that He would
guarantee his restoration (38:14).

The second stanza of Hezekiah's song of thanksgiving reflects
the gratitude and delight of the king at Yahweh's having restored
him (38:15-20). His joy made him at a loss for words. Yahweh
had not only promised his deliverance, but He had actually brought
it to pass (38:15a). Therefore, Hezekiah would "go softly" (in
humility?) because of the lessons he had learned from his recent
experience (38:15b).

Hezekiah continued, "by these things men live" — it is by the
deeds and benefits of Yahweh that men live (38:16). In love
Yahweh had reached into the pit (death) and had lifted Hezekiah
from it; and in so doing He had consigned his sins to oblivion
(38:17b). Thus, the king realized that the suffering which he had
endured in reality had been of great benefit to him. Men could
not praise Yahweh in Sheol. But Hezekiah was still among the
living, and He would praise Yahweh as long as He permitted him
to live (38:18-20). Then verse 21 states the physical means used
by Yahweh to heal the "boil." This was probably a sore which
was symptomatic of the plague, and it may even have been an indication that recovery was possible. Regardless of the exact nature of
the illness, this thought was clear — Yahweh was responsible for all
that had happened and Hezekiah was the first to acknowledge it.

6. *Babylon's Embassy to Jerusalem* (39:1-8). Merodach-
baladan, king of Babylon, upon learning of Hezekiah's illness and
subsequent recovery, sent the king some important letters along with
a present (39:1). Probably the letters contained a proposal that
the two of them join forces in revolt against Assyria. Hezekiah
was flattered by the attention shown him as well as by the offer
which had been made. The plot was in keeping with his own think-
ing. So, in order to impress the embassy with his strength, he
showed them all the resources of the kingdom (39:2). In all likelihood, this was for the purpose of guaranteeing his own acceptable-
ness in case such an undertaking came to pass.

This display of pride and folly did not escape the attention of
Isaiah, who had suspected intrigue from the start (39:3). He in-

quired concerning the purpose of the embassy and the country from which it had been sent. Hezekiah answered unhesitatingly. Then Isaiah declared that the day would come that all of Judah would be taken into captivity. Because of Hezekiah's planned reliance upon Babylon rather than a confident trust in Yahweh for protection and deliverance, the nation could not expect to survive Yahweh's disfavor. Hezekiah responded in verse 8, displaying his resignation to the prophet's announcement as he said, "Good is the word of Jehovah which thou hast spoken." Then he added, "For there shall be peace and truth in my days." Although this verse is difficult to interpret, it may mean that Yahweh's judgment would be tempered with mercy. If so, then Yahweh's mercy would be exhibited by a delay in the arrival of the punishment.

### FOR FURTHER STUDY OR DISCUSSION

1. Read article on "Hezekiah" in IDB, Volume II, pp. 598-600 and in ZPBD, p. 353.

2. Read article on "Rabshakeh" in IDB, Volume IV, p. 3 and in ZPBD, p. 702.

3. Read article on "Tirhakah" in IDB, Volume IV, p. 652 and in ZPBD, p. 856.

4. Do you believe political figures should seek the counsel of religious leaders in our day as Hezekiah did in his? Do they? If so, who are some of them? If not, why not?

5. Do political leaders heed the counsel of religious leaders today? If not, why not?

6. What impressed you most about Hezekiah's illness and recovery?

7. What example did Hezekiah leave for you after his recovery?

CHAPTER 9

# God's Plan for the Ages

(Isaiah 40-48)

1. *The Prologue* (40:1-31)
2. *Yahweh's Challenge to the Nations and Their Gods* (41:1-29)
3. *The Servant of Yahweh* (42:1-25)
4. *A Creator Who Redeems* (43:1—44:23)
5. *Cyrus and the Opening of the Gates* (44:24—45:25)
6. *Babylon Sitting in the Dust and Salvation Set in Zion* (46:1—48:22)

With chapter 40 the emphasis of Isaiah turns to comfort and assurance. Most commentators claim that the material found in this part of the book is concerned primarily with the return from exile, and that some of it was written shortly before the restoration and some of it later. There is a second method of approach to this section, the one taken by fewer commentators. Those who hold this view insist that Isaiah wrote these chapters during his later life and not solely for the purpose of comforting those in exile. They contend that this section also shows the circumstances of the Messiah's appearing and the future conditions of a spiritual Israel. Whichever position one may hold, he finds himself dealing with a most remarkable section. There is nothing else in the Old Testament to compare with it. It must be stated, however, that it is involved and difficult, and it is not easy to treat chapter by chapter.

This section opens with a prologue which sets forth the basic concepts. These concepts appear again and again in chapter after chapter.

1. *The Prologue* (40:1-31). Chapter 40 begins with an announcement of comfort for those in exile. It is interesting to compare this chapter with the first chapter in the book of Isaiah. There is

a sharp contrast between the past condition of Judah and the future of glorious promises!

Verses 1 and 2 announce the approach of a new day for the exiles. It is a day in which "her warfare" will be over (the expiration of the period of punishment because of her sin), and when "her iniquity" will be pardoned (when her guilt is taken care of, as when a debt is paid in full). This day will signal the preparation for the restoration (40:3-5). The angelic hosts will appear and rid the way of every obstacle for those returning. The valleys will "be exalted" and the mountains and hills "made low." The rough and uneven places would be smoothed. Nothing will prevent Yahweh's realizing His purpose in the restoration of His people from Babylon.

The prophet called attention to the frailty and transitoriness of man (40:6, 7). He stated that there was not much in man that encouraged hopefulness. Yet, he reassured his hearers by declaring that the promises of the future did not depend upon man but upon the sure word of Yahweh (40:8). By reflecting such assurance Isaiah was simply saying, "Yahweh's purpose in the world cannot and will not be thwarted by natural means nor by human limitation and frailty." These promises were so certain of realization that the prophet was told to announce the approach of Yahweh and His people from the exile (40:9). He was instructed to say "Behold your God!" when he saw them coming toward the city. By such an announcement the prophet encouraged the people to remember that the restoration will be accomplished by Yahweh despite all opposition.

Such positive assurance was based upon the nature and character of Yahweh. He was not just another god. He was the "mighty one" whose arm (the symbol of strength) would rule in authority (40:10a) as well as in fairness and justice (40:10b). He would exercise all the prerogatives and all the tender care of a shepherd as He brought His own back from exile (40:11). Then, as though attempting to persuade any who might doubt Yahweh's ability to accomplish His intent for those to be restored, the prophet continued with a detailed characterization of Him (40:12-31).

Yahweh was the creator of all that man could see and know (40:12). At the time of creation He had used the care of one weighing out the precise amount of ingredients to go into a mixture. There was just the right amount of everything in all which Yahweh had created (40:12). He had created this universe independently (40:13). He did not need nor did He receive any direction or counsel. He was omniscient (40:14). All the nations of the earth were but a "drop in a bucket" or the unnoticed dust on a balance when compared to Yahweh (40:15-17). His greatness was of such degree that if Lebanon were an altar and its trees wood for the sacrificial fire, all her animals would not be sufficient to make a worthy sacrifice to Him (40:16).

Nothing in creation can be compared to its Creator (40:18-21). He could not be likened to the creations of man, be they ever so god-like, because He was the sovereign in control of man and nature (who "sitteth above the circle of the earth") (40:22-26). He was the everlasting God who supplied the needs of life, despite all the demands for strength and help made upon Him by frail man (He "fainteth not, neither is weary") (40:27-31). When men "wait for Jehovah," they are borne along and sustained by faith and hope in the same way in which the eagle is borne aloft by its wings or the walker or runner is sustained by a second wind.

What words of comfort and consolation these were. How incomparable the God of Israel! What bright promises for the future!

2. *Yahweh's Challenge to the Nations and Their Gods* (41:1-29). Yahweh called for a convocation of the nations to consider the remarkable rise of Cyrus and his equally remarkable overthrow of kingdom after kingdom (41:1-3). How could this be explained? What had brought it to pass? The triumph of Cyrus was the work of Yahweh Himself (41:4).

Because of the unrest created by the Persian victories the nations of the earth turned to their neighbors for help, seeking new gods who could give them some form of encouragement (41:5, 6). But these efforts would prove futile, for these gods could neither hear nor respond to need. Rather, they had to be secured so that they would not fall apart nor topple to the ground. They had no strength in themselves; therefore, it was vain to seek their counsel (41:7).

In verses 8-20 the scene moves to Israel. She did not need to be afraid of conditions in the world because she had been chosen to be Yahweh's servant and He would help her (41:8-10). Those who had been her enemies and who had held her people captive were going to be made powerless, and ultimately disappear (41:11-13). Therefore, Yahweh's covenant people were not to fear. His own help guarantees their accomplishing His purpose for them. They will be delivered from their captors and returned to the land from which they had been taken.

During the time in which she was being strengthened, Israel was to serve as a sharp threshing instrument by which God would mete out divine judgment in the world (41:14-16). The allusion to Israel as "thou worm Jacob" is strange. It perhaps refers to Israel's limitation in size; and in this case, it possibly is a term of love and appreciation for the nation.

The next paragraph (verses 17-20) reiterates the assurances found in Yahweh's promises to Israel. He will provide her with every necessity. Even the barren desert will be supplied with water and become forests in anticipation of her needs. When the nations behold these miraculous events, they will know that these wonders were His work and they learn a great lesson comparing Yahweh with their own helpless gods.

Verses 21-29 are a continuation of Jehovah's contempt for the gods of the nations. They were challenged to prove in any way possible — give one evidence or one sign, either good or bad — that they could explain the meaning of what was happening. But they could not. Therefore, He called them nothing and their worshipers abominable.

In vivid contrast to these gods, these nothings, Yahweh knew what was happening because it was He who had "raised up one" (Cyrus) (41:25, 26). He was in control.

3. *The Servant of Yahweh* (42:1-25). The prophet added another theme — the Servant of Yahweh — to the list of those already introduced. In this section, the character and function of the Servant are discussed. Israel was the Servant who was to be redeemed from Babylon that she might be a blessing to all men. Even though she had failed to measure up to her privileges and opportunities, Yahweh's purpose would be accomplished in spite of her.

(a) THE SERVANT INTRODUCED AND COMMISSIONED (42:1-9). Saying that the Servant in this passage was Israel is quite different from saying that Israel fulfilled the role of the Servant — most agree that she did not. Quite the contrary seems to be the case. Yet, it must be contended that although the nation did not accomplish the goals of the Servant, One from the nation did. Through the Messiah, the purposes of Yahweh for all Israel came to be realized.

The Servant was introduced by Yahweh who had set him apart for a special mission and had endowed him with His own Spirit (42:1). This election was for the purpose of bringing "forth justice to the nations." Through his ministry and lack of prejudice He will establish true worship in the earth, fulfilling the conditions set out in 2:1-4.

The ministry of the Servant was to be characterized by its relative quiet (42:2). His accomplishments come through the gentle, yet strong, spiritual forces of Yahweh. Through his approach, He strengthens and encourages the people. He does not contribute to the expiration of goodness and justice, which was at least implied in the reference to "a bruised reed and dimly burning wick" (42:3).

Verse 4 states that the Servant will not "burn dimly" nor "be broken." He is not beset by the afflictions of those He had come to aid, nor does He fail to reveal His truth. If the last clause of the verse is translated "do wait" instead of "shall wait," and some suggest the possibility, then the idea may well be that the nations of the earth had not found the satisfaction longed for in their kind of faith and are waiting hopefully for a faith which does satisfy.

The Servant had been called for a purpose that was righteous and will be given . . . "for a covenant of the people, for a light of the Gentiles . . ." (42:5, 6). The idea of the Servant's being "a covenant of the people" means that he will be the basis of the covenant upon which Israel would build her future. He will also be "a light to the Gentiles." Through that covenant He offers light and hope to those in spiritual blindness or spiritual bondage (42:7).

Verses 8-9 shift the emphasis from the Servant to the Master. Jehovah declared that He will not allow the glory which was due Him to go to another (42:8). The "former things" which Yahweh had predicted had already come to pass; therefore, the "new things" which He declared will also come to pass (42:9). These "new things" of which Yahweh spoke are the work of the Servant, the restoration of Israel, and the bringing of the nations to Him. The people are to believe that these will come to pass as surely as the "former things" had.

(b) PRAISE TO YAHWEH WHOSE WORK IT IS (42:10-17). With the mention of "new things" the prophet announced a "new song," and he called for it to be sung from one end of the earth to the other by every creature and every object upon the earth (42:10-12). They are to give praise to Yahweh because He will go forth to do battle against His enemies and will prevail (42:13). Yahweh will not be defeated in the carrying out of His purpose in the world. He will do mightily.

Verse 14 describes the Lord's role in the past. He had been

silent (inactive) for a long time. But He had restrained Himself as long as He could. He would cry out, as a woman giving birth, because He could no longer be deterred in His will and purpose (42: 14). The breath of His anger will make the most luxuriant areas as dry and as barren as a desert (42:15). Even so, Yahweh will not be turned away from His intention to deliver the exiles. He will lead those who could not find their way over paths which they could not themselves locate (42:16). And through Yahweh's mighty deed, the Babylonians, who trusted in idols, will be put to utter shame (42:17).

(c) THE FAILURE OF ISRAEL AS THE SERVANT (42:18-25). The people of Israel were admonished to turn their eyes upon their past responses to opportunities for serving Yahweh. They had responded as men "blind" to their responsibility and "deaf" to His voice (42:19). The question, "Who is blind but my servant?" implies that Israel's blindness was greater than that of any nation. She, who was "at peace" with Yahweh and who had been perfectly equipped by Him, was the blindest of all nations. Israel had not comprehended the significance of the "many things" which Yahweh had done on her behalf (42:20). Yahweh had planned to establish His righteousness and His teachings by sharing them with all nations. Israel had not recognized His purpose and evidently was not about to (42:21, 22).

Out of such a sober context the prophet called for some of the people to realize the possibilities for them in Yahweh's purpose for the future (42:23). Surely what Yahweh had brought upon them should have taught them the folly of resisting His purpose (42:24). Yet they had not taken it to heart (42:25).

4. *A Creator Who Redeems* (43:1—44:23). Israel, who had failed so tragically in the past, was told to be unafraid of the future because the One who had created her would redeem her.

(a) YAHWEH'S PURPOSE TO REDEEM ISRAEL (43:1-7). Israel, who had been created by Yahweh and chosen as His own, was going to be redeemed from every danger, in this case "water" and "fire," which are symbols of the gravest dangers (43:1, 2). Many believe the point of verse 3 is that Cyrus — who received Egypt, Ethiopia and Seba (a province in Ethiopia) from Yahweh, along with all the remainder of Babylon's possessions — received them as ransom for Israel. Because of His relationship with Israel, Yahweh will restore every one of His sons and daughters (43:4-7).

(b) ISRAEL AS A WITNESS (43:8-13). The prophet, imagining a scene in which the nations were assembled, heard Yahweh call for those nations to bear witness as to whether they were able to declare the truth of 43:1-7. They were either to accept the true meaning of Yahweh's purpose through Cyrus or give evidence that they were right in not doing so (43:8, 9). The nations and their gods were unable to deny the prediction of deliverance for Israel and the fact that Yahweh had the power to bring it to pass. Yahweh then declared that Israel, herself, was a witness and an evidence of His power to make known the future as well as to bring to pass that which had been made known (43:10-13).

(c) THE FALL OF BABYLON AND THE DELIVERANCE OF ISRAEL (43:14-21). The redemption of Israel will begin with the downfall of Babylon. The people of Babylon were going to be taken captive and transported down the Euphrates on the same ships in which they once sailed for joy and pleasure (43:14).

Because of who He is, Yahweh will repeat what He had done against the Egyptians. He will even surpass what He had done to the Egyptians at the time of the first exodus (43:17-19). On the day of the second exodus, Yahweh will provide a highway through a desert which would have been transformed by rivers of water. As he leads His people along the way there will be no need to fear the creatures of the wilderness, because even they will defer to the person and purpose of Yahweh (43:19, 20). As a result of these acts of goodness on Yahweh's part, Israel will praise Him in joy and gratitude (43:21).

(d) ISRAEL'S DELIVERANCE WAS FOR YAHWEH'S SAKE (43:22-28). It is not because of Israel's ready response to Yahweh's promise of help that He will deliver her. Rather than responding favorably, she had grown weary of Him (43:22). Yahweh had not burdened Israel with unreasonable sacrifices and offerings (43:23), and yet she had burdened Him with her sins (43:24). Therefore, there was nothing about Israel which called for any act of grace on Yahweh's part. If Israel were to be spared, it would be for Yahweh's sake and not for her own (43:25).

In verses 26-27 Yahweh challenged Israel to present her case in order that she might be justified. He reminded her that her father (Jacob) and her religious leaders had sinned; and thus, by implication, the entire population had sinned. Therefore, Yahweh will bring judgment upon the cities and their people (43:28).

(e) YAHWEH'S SPIRIT FOR HIS CHOSEN ONES (44:1-8). Now the emphasis shifts from the dark picture of 43:27, 28 to the glorious prospects of the future. Jacob and Jeshurun (a synonym for Israel) were encouraged to be unafraid, for they were His chosen ones (44:1, 2). He will provide for them and protect them. A new nation will be established. Yahweh will pour out His Spirit upon Israel and her offspring until they are as great in number as the blades of grass along the water courses. When that occurs the nations will come and cast their lot with the new Israel, even to the point of wearing her name (44:3-5).

Verses 6-8 take up the theme previously discussed in which Yahweh claimed that He alone was God. "There is no Rock . . ." beside Him.

(f) THE FUTILITY OF IDOLS (44:9-23). The gods which frail men made and delighted in profit them nothing (44:9-11). Despite all the effort expended by the workmen and all the care they employed in their task, that which they produced is of so little value as a god that it would have profited them more had they used the wood for fire (44:12-17). Yet, those who fell down before these idols to worship were so infatuated with them that they never stopped to consider how futile their efforts really were (44:18-20).

In verse 21, Israel was admonished to take the truths about idolatry to heart and remember that she was Jehovah's servant who would never be forgotten by Him (44:21). To give evidence of His faithfulness, Yahweh reminded her of His grace. Just when Israel thought she had been forgotten, Yahweh announced that He had forgiven her sins and invited her to return to Him (44:21, 22). Because of this good news heaven and earth were called "to break forth into singing . . . for Jehovah hath redeemed Jacob, and will glorify himself in Israel" (44:23).

5. *Cyrus and the Opening of the Gate* (44:24—45:25). At the outset of this remarkable passage, Yahweh identified Himself as the Creator of the Universe and the God of Prophecy who can overcome all that militates against His purpose and who will use every opportunity to enhance it.

(a) YAHWEH'S PURPOSE THROUGH CYRUS (44:24—45:8). Yahweh, the sole Creator, will frustrate all idolatrous prognostications and bring to pass all that He had promised for Israel in the days to come (44:24-26). Whatever might appear to be in the way will be abolished — "the deep" is an example or symbol of the obstacles which the restoration would encounter (44:27). Yahweh will even go so far as to use Cyrus to accomplish His purpose (44:28). Through the defeat of Babylon and the granting of freedom to the captives, Cyrus will be performing the work of Yahweh's "shepherd." In this case, "shepherd" means "ruler" or "administrator." Cyrus will then be Yahweh's administrator who will set the captives free and order the rebuilding of Jerusalem and the Temple.

In 45:1 Cyrus is referred to as Yahweh's "anointed," the only occasion on which a foreign ruler was so designated. It simply means that Cyrus was one set aside by Yahweh to carry out a specific assignment. The commission of Cyrus entailed the conquest of the nations which stood in the way of Yahweh's purposes (45: 2, 3), which were the restoration and exaltation of Israel and the universal recognition of Himself as the only God (45:4-7). He was the one who formed the "light" and created "darkness;" He made "peace" and created "evil" (used here to mean physical disaster. Cf. Amos 3:6); He was Yahweh, "that doeth all these things."

Verse 8 contains a prophetic plea that heaven and earth be enlisted and encouraged to bring forth the salvation and the righteousness of Yahweh.

(b) THE OPPOSITION TO YAHWEH'S PURPOSE THROUGH CYRUS (45:9-13). Some of those who heard the prophet's announcement reacted negatively to the fact that Yahweh was using Cyrus to accomplish His purpose. In the face of this reaction, the prophet pronounced the woes of verses 9-10. He condemned such people through the use of the figures of the potter and the clay and the parent and the child. Just as it would be folly for a piece of pottery to challenge the potter, so would it be folly for frail man to challenge his maker (45:9). Just as it would be effrontery for a child to castigate his parents for bringing him into the world, so would it be effrontery for men to challenge the purposes of Yahweh.

In the remaining verses of this section, the prophet delivered Yahweh's response to those who had challenged Him (45:11-13). Yahweh declared that He had made all things and was in authority over all things; therefore, He had raised up Cyrus in accordance with His sovereign purpose. He had done so that His people might go free and that His city might be rebuilt. He had sought no counsel nor would He accept any.

(c) YAHWEH THE ONLY HOPE FOR ISRAEL AND THE NATIONS (45:14-25). With verse 14, the prophet turns to a description of the conditions which will result from Cyrus' work. The nations — those who were to be the "ransom" for Israel (see 43:3) and who were conquered by Cyrus — will turn to Israel and prostrate themselves before her. In so doing, they will be acknowledging Yahweh's abiding purpose for Israel. But they will also be acknowledging Israel as a mediator through whom they might express their acceptance of Yahweh. Up to that time Yahweh will not have revealed Himself to them through the work of restoration, so their response will be "thou art a God that hidest thyself, O God of Israel, the Saviour" (45:15).

In verses 16 and 17 the prophet contrasts the future conditions of the nations with those of Israel.

In Verse 18 Yahweh declares that He did not create the world that it might be uninhabited, but that men might dwell in it. Since that was His purpose, a way must be provided for Him to accomplish it. That way is salvation. He contends that He had "not spoken in secret, in a place of the land of darkness." When the world seeks Him, as He called upon them to do, He intends to be available. When He speaks "righteousness," He intends to stand by His word (45:19).

The remnants of the nations will be called together and asked who had foretold the events of Cyrus' victory (45:20, 21). They will learn that it was Yahweh. They then will be admonished to look to Him from every corner of the earth, and all will be saved who will acknowledge His sovereignty and acts of righteousness (45:22-25).

6. *Babylon Sitting in the Dust and Salvation Set in Zion* (46: 1—48:22). This section deals primarily with the contrast between Yahweh and the idols of Babylon and between the circumstances of the restored Israel and those of Babylon.

(a) BABYLON'S IDOLS CONTRASTED WITH ISRAEL'S YAHWEH (46:1-13). At the outset of chapter 46 the prophet described the attempts of the Babylonians to save their gods from the Persians. Bel was the head of the Babylonian pantheon, and Nebo was his son. They both fell prostrate. They would not be borne away to safety (46:1, 2). But Yahweh, who had borne His people from the beginning will bear them for all the future (46:3, 4). How foolish it was for men to depend upon gods which had to be borne about by their worshipers and which were as nothing when compared with Yahweh (46:5-7).

With verse 8, the prophet appealed to the past and to the revelation of Yahweh in history as evidence that He would accomplish all that He purposed for the future (46:8-11). Therefore, they were admonished to repent because salvation was soon to be established in Zion (46:12, 13).

(b) YAHWEH'S JUDGMENT UPON BABYLON (47:1-15). Babylon, characterized as a virgin (unconquered) resplendently enthroned, is ordered to leave her throne and sit on the ground in humiliation (47:1). Her people will take upon themselves the work of the lowliest slave when they are sent into exile (47:2). Yahweh will not spare one man among them because of the abuse Babylon had heaped upon those He delivered into her hands and because of her boasting that her rule would last forever (47:3-7).

The proud and boastful nation, which had entertained visions of abiding grandeur and superiority, will know the sorrows of "widowhood" and "loss of children" in a sudden and unexpected moment (47:8, 9). The reason for her bigotry was that her people had great knowledge of such subjects as astrology and sorcery (47:10). But this will bring a judgment upon them which they will not be able to ward off with their charms and incantations (47:11, 12).

Verses 12-15 show the futility of Babylon's practices. In her condition, there will be no way for her to be saved.

(c) ISRAEL'S OBSTINACY REBUKED AND HER DELIVERANCE PROMISED (48:1-22). The first paragraph of chapter 48 relates Yahweh's method of dealing with Israel and the lessons taught by this method. In verse 1, Yahweh was commanding the attention of Israel that she might hear the oracle which He was going to proclaim (beginning with verse 3). The people of Israel claimed to be the people of Yahweh, but they had not acted as though they were (48:1, 2). Yahweh had predicted events which were going to come to pass so that they might realize that these things were of Himself and not of the idols (48:3-5). In doing this, Yahweh was establishing His ability to predict and was also preparing the nation for "new things" to come (6-8). He realized that Israel had not acted as though she were His. She deserved to be destroyed, and she would have been but for His commitment to honor His name (48:9-11).

Because of Yahweh's regard for His name, He planned to deal with the Chaldeans and He revealed His intention beforehand (48:12-16). He began by identifying Himself as the only God (48:12).

He was the creator of all the universe (48:13). In light of His power and purpose, Yahweh announced His intention through Cyrus and He assured the people of Israel that this purpose was going to be realized (48:14-16).

Had Israel responded to Him in the past, her present would have been quite different (48:18, 19). Instead of being in exile, she would have been in righteousness and at peace. "Peace" here refers to an abundant prosperity for the nation. "Righteousness" refers to the establishment of the divine "right," or salvation with all its attendant benefits. Yahweh was saying: "Had you responded to Me, you would not be as you now are. You would have lived in peace and righteousness and your progeny would have been as great in number of the sands of the sea."

Despite Israel's rejection of Yahweh's offer in the past and her present tragic condition, Yahweh, for His name's sake, will redeem her through the work of Cyrus. Therefore, her people were admonished to sing that Yahweh was the Redeemer as they left the confines of Babylon (48:20). They were to leave in all confidence because they will know the same provisions and security, which they had known in the wilderness of Sinai. But the wicked will not know any of these blessings of the redeemed (48:21, 22).

### FOR FURTHER STUDY OR DISCUSSION

1. What differences do you see between Isaiah 1-39 and Isaiah 40-66?

2. Have you thought of the exile as a time of purifying the nation?

3. Read the article on "The Servant of the Lord" in IDB, Volume IV, pp. 292-294.

4. Did the failure of Israel mean Jehovah's purpose through the nation had failed? If not, what did it mean? How would the purpose be realized?

5. If the deliverance of Israel was for Jehovah's sake what does this imply for all His benefits?

6. Read article on "Cyrus" in IDB, Volume I, pp. 754, 755 and in ZPBD, p. 193.

7. Does God still use international figures who do not believe in Him to accomplish His own ends? Can you suggest possible examples?

8. Are the contrasts between Jehovah and the idols of Babylon still valid in a consideration of the gods which modern men have? What other differences would you suggest?

# CHAPTER 10

# The Servant,
# the Agent of Salvation

(Isaiah 49-55)

This chapter deals with the two basic themes found in Isaiah 49-55. The first presents the Servant as the agent of Yahweh's salvation. The second pertains to the effect of the Servant's work upon the world.

The identity of the Servant has been the source of much discussion. It seems quite clear that the identity of the Servant in 42:1 ff. is Israel. As to the remaining Servant passages, however, there are those who contend that the Servant is the Messiah or the ideal (true) Israel. Perhaps the matter is best approached by showing the development from one Servant poem to the other. In the first poem (42:1-4), it is generally agreed that the Servant is the nation. But as one moves from the first poem to the second (49:1-6) it seems that the Servant is one who is to restore Israel (49:5, 6); therefore, He could not *be* Israel. The two remaining poems, though all do not agree, are to be taken here as referring to the Messiah.

1. *The Commissioning of the Servant* (49:1-26). This section in Isaiah begins with what is generally called the second Servant poem (49:1-6). (The position taken here is that the Servant is the Messiah, not the nation.)

(a) THE SERVANT'S ANNOUNCEMENT (49:1-6). Chapter 49

opens with the announcement of the Servant's mission to all the nations. He had been called into existence ("from the womb") so that the nations might hear Yahweh's purpose (49:1). In order that all will realize the importance of that which He had come to do, He is identified as *Yahweh's Servant*. He had been concealed by the hand of Yahweh until the divinely-appointed time (49:2), and during that period of concealment had been equipped with a mouth "like a sharp sword," (the capacity to speak formidably for Yahweh). Too, He was Yahweh's "polished shaft," held in readiness for battle against the enemy.

In verse 3, if "Israel" is to be taken as "my servant," then the idea is that Yahweh will glorify Himself in His Servant Israel. Yet verse 4 presents a problem at this point because His purpose with Israel had not been the rewarding experience He had planned it should be. Israel had to be brought to Yahweh by the Servant. This being the case, the nation cannot be the Servant but is to be brought to Yahweh *by* the Servant (49:5).

If this is a valid approach to the identity of the Servant, then this poem provides the transition from the nation as the Servant to one of that nation whose mission it was to bring the nation to Yahweh. The Servant is an individual Israelite, through whom Yahweh would accomplish that which He had planned for Israel among the nations of the earth (49:6). Through one out of Israel, Yahweh will not only realize His purpose in Israel, but He will accomplish His intention for the nations as well. In both cases, His purpose was salvation.

(b) THE RESULTS OF THE SERVANT'S COMMISSIONING (49: 7-13). The role of the Servant involves several things. Two of these — the effect of the Servant upon the nations, and His work as the restorer of Israel — are contained in this section. When the rulers of the earth understand Yahweh's plan for the world, they will do Him homage (49:7).

Another emphasis (49:8-13) deals with the restoration of Israel. Yahweh pledged Himself to "preserve" Israel and to give her "for a covenant of the people." Israel is the means through which the nations would be brought to Yahweh. When the time for the restoration arrived, those returning will be adequately cared for. They will come from every part of the earth, from as far away as "Syene," modern Aswan. Because of these words of promise and hope, both heaven and earth were called upon to sing and rejoice (49:13).

(c) DEJECTED ZION ASSURED OF YAHWEH'S LOVE (49:14-26). Though Zion may have believed herself forsaken, Yahweh will no more forget her than a woman could forget her young child. It is more likely that a mother would forget her child than that Yahweh would forget Israel (49:14, 15)! To assure Himself that He will not forget the nation, Yahweh sketched a plan for the restored community upon the palms of His hands (49:16). In his vision the prophet could see the exiles returning (49:17, 18). The signs of widowhood gave way to the ornaments of a bride and the desolate places were repopulated by numbers too great for the area to accommodate (49:19, 20). Then, in bewilderment Zion asked how these things can come to pass (49:21). As though answering the question, Yahweh stated that at His signal the nations will not only make possible the return of the exiles to their homes but they will also humble themselves before the restored Israel in self-humiliation (49:22, 23). Yahweh revealed that no nation, however mighty or terrible it might be, can restrain His people (49:25). Instead of affecting Israel, they will destroy themselves through revolution and strife (49:26). When that happens, men will know of the might and power of Yahweh and the indestructible nature of His purpose for Israel.

2. *The Servant's Confidence in Yahweh* (50:1-11). The paragraphs or divisions of chapter 50 are diverse. Verses 1-3 contain a reference to Israel's bill of divorcement; verses 4-9, the third Servant poem; and verses 10-11, a word of encouragement and warning based upon the previous division.

(a) ISRAEL'S BILL OF DIVORCEMENT (50:1-3). Israel, because of her rebellion against Yahweh, feared a permanent separation from her covenant God. To allay her fears Yahweh asked for the bill of divorcement, and in so doing implied that no such decree existed (50:1a). He asked for the name of the creditor to whom He had sold her as payment of a debt. This signified that He was debtor to no man and that He would on no grounds sell His own into slavery (50:1b). Yahweh then proceeded to clarify the causes of the exile (50:1c). The people's suffering was due to their iniquity and transgression. When Yahweh did offer them hope through the prophet, there was "no man . . . to answer" or respond (50:2a). But this did not mean that Yahweh was limited, because the whole world of nature would prove Him to be otherwise (50:2b, 3).

(b) THE SERVANT AND HIS SUFFERING (50:4-9). In this passage the Servant was characterized as having a disciple's tongue; He was taught by Yahweh that He might know how "to sustain" or silence those who were wearied by the conditions and circumstances of their lives (50:4a). Day by day, morning by morning, He yielded an attentive ear to the voice of His Teacher (50:4b). He learned from that voice the necessity of faithfulness to the will of Yahweh and the Servant did not, therefore, rebel against Yahweh's direction (50:5). Even though the will of Yahweh led to persecution the Servant would pursue the assigned way. That way ultimately resulted in the Servant's being smitten and humiliated; His persecutors plucked out His beard and spat upon Him in contempt and disrespect (50:6).

Even though persecution was the lot of the Servant, He was able to endure the hardships of His experience because of His assurance of help from Yahweh (50:7). Then as though the Servant were a disputant in a legal procedure, He asked who would dare challenge Him with Yahweh at hand to declare Him right. Those who condemn the Servant and who had done such harm in the past will finally decay as an old garment, or perish as clothing eaten by the moths (50:8, 9). The Servant will inevitably succeed while those opposed to Him will inevitably fail!

(b) A WORD OF HOPE AND WARNING (50:10, 11). In verse 10, hope is extended to those who trust in "the name of Jehovah, and rely upon his God." Those who depended upon Yahweh as had the Servant, have every reason to anticipate light (salvation) in exchange for the darkness (distress) they had known so long. Those who refuse to look at Him kindle their own fires of destruction (50:11).

3. *Yahweh's Past Care the Earnest of the Future* (51:1—52:12). Those left in Zion were instructed to look to the quarry ("rock whence ye were hewn"). The quarry is their ancestors. They were to look to them and take heart as they realized that their forebears, too, were a part of Yahweh's all-encompassing purpose.

(a) YAHWEH AND ABRAHAM (51:1-3). Those remaining in Zion were to find comfort in that which Yahweh had accomplished through Abraham and Sarah (51:2). He had taken this one couple, and from them He had brought the multitudes of Israel into existence. He plans the same for those left in Zion since they are the inheritors of Yahweh's promise to Abraham. In addition, the barren earth will again be made productive and the land will once more ring with the joy of thanksgiving as a result of Yahweh's faithfulness (51:3).

(b) LAW AND SALVATION (51:4-8). The law of Yahweh, received at the time of Moses, will reap dividends in the future as it had in the past. The law, which is the basis of justice in the world, will be "for a light of the peoples" (51:4). In view of Yahweh's rescue of Israel from her captors, all nations will look to Him for deliverance and a new way of life (51:5). In that day, the present "heavens" and "earth" will give way to new ones in which His salvation and righteousness will never cease (51:6).

Following these glowing promises, Israel was admonished to endure patiently the reproach of men and their revilings because the day of Yahweh's salvation will more than compensate for such abuse. It will be salvation which is eternal (51:7, 8).

(c) YAHWEH AND THE DAYS OF OLD (51:9-11). Either the prophet or the community, and possibly both, called upon Yahweh to demonstrate His strength as in the days of old, when He cut Rahab (the symbol of all opposed to Yahweh's purpose in creation) in pieces (51:9) and redeemed Israel from Egypt (51:10). As Yahweh had exercised His power in the past, He was petitioned to exercise it once more on Zion's behalf that her sorrow might give way to joy (51:11).

(d) YAHWEH AND HIS PEOPLE (51:12-16). In response to the appeal of verses 9-11, Yahweh told His people to be unafraid of that which men could do and remember the power of Yahweh who created all things (51:12, 13). Those in exile did not need to fear the fate of the forgotten prisoner. They will be restored despite all which seem to stand in the way (51:14, 15). The time of their restoration will be the day of the new creation (51:16).

(e) YAHWEH AND THE DRAINED BOWL (51:17—52:12). Jerusalem, having drunk the cup of Yahweh's indignation and having been left helpless by it, will see that same bitter cup passed to those who had afflicted her so long (51:17-23). Then Jerusalem will clothe herself in her robes of rejoicing (52:1, 2). Yahweh will bring her subjugation to an end (52:3-6) and restore her to Zion (52:7-12). He Himself will lead the pilgrimage back to the city, and when Zion hears the tidings of their approach she will break forth in joy.

4. *The Vicarious Nature of the Servant's Suffering* (52:13—53:12). This part of Isaiah is the best known of all the book.

Even so, there is no absolute agreement as to the identity of the Servant. The positions suggested earlier apply to this section as well. Generally, the position of Jewish scholars has been that the Servant is Israel, but the Christian community remains divided on the question. There are those who hold to the basic position of Jewish scholars, but maintain that the Servant refers to the "ideal" or "redeemed" Israel. Then, there are those who contend that the early church saw the fulfillment of these words in the life and death of Christ, and therefore, assert that these are references to the personal Messiah who suffered vicariously for the sins of the world. This passage will be examined in light of the last position.

(a) THE SERVANT INTRODUCED AND EXALTED (52:13-15). Although the mission of the Servant might appear to lack every promise of success, He will attain unto great heights. Although men, and even nations, were appalled at "his visage" and "his form" (His unusual appearance or His divergence from the ways of other men), He will prosper and succeed in His mission (52:13, 14). He will meet with such success that the nations will be "startled" (surprised) and their kings will be made speechless by His attainments (52:15a). They had received no word in advance of the Servant and the attainments of the Servant were unlike any ever before known (52: 15b). The world will be overwhelmed by the ultimate accomplishments of One who in the eyes of men showed so little promise.

(b) THE CAREER OF THE SERVANT AND ITS EFFECTS (53:1-9). Some have suggested that the speakers here are the kings mentioned in the preceding paragraph. Others are of the opinion that the speaker is the prophet. In either case, the role of the Servant remains the same.

The questions raised in the first verse were answered by implication: "No one believed what they had heard and no one had received an explanation." There were two reasons for their skepticism. First, there was the unattractive aspect of the Servant. His appearance was such that men did not care to look at Him (53:2). Second, He was despised and friendless, a man of pains and sickness from whom men will hide their faces. They would not look upon Him; they "esteemed Him not" (53:3).

Then, the speaker changed the emphasis. He saw that the Servant was bearing the pains and sickness of others — they were not His. He was wounded for the sins of the world (53:4, 5). All men had gone astray, each had turned his own way; but Yahweh made to light on him "the iniquity of us all" (53:6). He assumed the role given Him by Yahweh and bore that iniquity nobly and victoriously. As sheep silently marched to the slaughter or shearing, "so he opened not his mouth" (53:7). No one considered that His death was due to their own sins (53:8). He had done nothing Himself to deserve death, yet die He must (53:9). But ultimately He will prosper and be victorious, for His sufferings were a part of Yahweh's purpose. Yahweh will prolong His days and bring success to all His efforts (53:10); and because of His success, many will be made righteous (53:11). Then Yahweh will "divide him a portion with the great," and He will attain a position of exaltation comparable to that of the noblest of warriors (53:12). In that position, He will not only bear the sins of many but He will also make intercession for transgressors.

5. *The Future Glory and Inviolability of Yahweh's People* (54:1-17). Chapter 54, like some other sections in 40-66, provides a recapitulation of themes previously presented. The chapter has two sections: Verses 1-10 emphasize once more the re-union of Zion and Yahweh; verses 11-17 describe the results, both material and spiritual, of that relationship.

(a) THE RESTORATION OF ZION (54:1-10). Since Zion may be taken to represent Israel, the concept presented in this section pertains to the restoration of the exiles. Israel will be barren during the period of the exile, but that time of distress will end (54:1). When it is over, her offspring will be so numerous that they will have to increase the size of their tents to provide them shelter (54:2). They will occupy the areas of their former oppressors and also those regions which had been so long uninhabited (54:3).

The future for Zion holds such promise that she will forget her former distress and shame (54:4), because her Maker and Redeemer will be her husband and will acknowledge her as His wife (54:5, 6). The separation between them will end; it will be but a brief period until it is overcome by His mercy (54:7, 8). Then there will be a relationship as permanent as Yahweh's promise to Noah; it will outlast the mountains. His "lovingkindness" and His "covenant of peace" will never again be withdrawn (54:9, 10).

(b) THE GLORIES OF RESTORED ZION (54:11-17). In figurative language the city is depicted as one made of "precious stones" (54:11, 12). The children there will be taught about Yahweh, and great peace and righteousness will result from their experiences

(54:13, 14). In that day, those who come against the city will not be sent by Yahweh as before, and, hence they will not succeed (54:15). Zion will no longer need fear her enemies, for their weapons and plans will fail them (54:16, 17). She will be securely established, and her relationship with Yahweh will be as happy and joyful as that of those newly wed.

6. *The World Invited to Eat That Which is Good* (55:1-13). With this chapter the climax of 40-55 is reached. Because of Yahweh's lavish provisions, all men are invited to be partakers in the blessings of the Messianic Age.

(a) THE INVITATION TO THE BANQUET (55:1-5). Those who are hungry and thirsty are promised complete satisfaction if they join the great banquet set before them (55:1-3). Men have spent so much for that which left them unsatisfied. They are now invited to the banquet of the Lord, and they will find it a delight to their souls. This figure telling of the freeness of Yahweh's salvation and the satisfaction which comes to the recipient.

In verses 4-5 the leader is Yahweh's Messiah. He is a witness to the great work and grace of Yahweh. Nations will, therefore, turn to Israel in hope and with confidence. They will rest in the assurance that they will not be led astray. They believed they will be satisfied.

(b) THE CALL TO REPENTANCE (55:5-9). Along with the invitation to the great banquet was the call to come to Yahweh in repentance because He will "abundantly pardon" (55:6, 7). All men need His pardon and may through His grace receive it. The kingdom of Yahweh is near and men need to meet the conditions of citizenship. It is a loftier ideal and concept than man can comprehend (55:8, 9), but Yahweh will bring it to pass.

(c) THE EXTENT OF THE KINGDOM (55:10-13). Just as the rain accomplishes its purpose as it falls upon the earth, so will the Word of Yahweh accomplish His purpose (55:10, 11). The Word is the expression of His purpose, and that which He purposed will be realized. Since His immediate plan for Israel is restoration, she can rest assured that she will return with Yahweh as her guide. The whole of the natural order will be transformed, and that miracle will be a perpetual memorial to the accomplishments of Yahweh on behalf of His own.

A careful reading of the book of Isaiah should make it clear that the prophet associated the restoration with the Messianic Age.

It will be a time when the Messiah would rule over the New Israel of God. Although the prophet did not live to experience that rule, in the fullness of time God brought it into existence through the reign of His Son, the promised Messiah.

### FOR FURTHER STUDY OR DISCUSSION

1. Do you agree that the second Servant passage is the transition from the nation to the individual? If you do not, why not?
2. Do God's past dealings suggest the direction of His future dealings? If so, what are the implications for the present? If not, why not?
3. Read article on "Suffering and Evil" in IDB, Volume IV, pp. 451-453.
4. Does Isaiah seem to equate the restoration with the atoning work of the Servant and the future glory of Zion? What are the implications of this?
5. Were the blessings of the Messianic Age to have been received by all men? How do you explain the exclusivism of the Jews? Is exclusivism still a problem for the people of God? If so, in what way?
6. According to Isaiah, what was to be the extent of Jehovah's kingdom? Has that purpose changed?

CHAPTER 11

# The Light of a New Day, the Glory of a New Era

(Isaiah 56-66)

1. *The Exhortation to Righteousness* (56:1—59:21)
2. *The Everlasting Glory of the New Jerusalem* (60:1-22)
3. *The Purpose and the Effect of the Servant's Mission* (61:1-11)
4. *The Determination of the Servant to Succeed* (62:1—63:6)
5. *The Prayer of Israel for Mercy and Help* (63:7—64:12)
6. *The New Heavens and the New Earth* (65:1—66:24)

Isaiah 56-66 is the last major division of the book. This section consists of exhortations to righteousness and promises of unparalleled glory for the future.

1. *The Exhortation to Righteousness* (56:1—59:21). Chapters 56-59 comprise that portion of Isaiah 40-66 which contrasts the condition of the righteous with the state of those who practice iniquity. Here we see the elimination of old restrictions and the gracious intervention of Yahweh to save all who were a part of spiritual Israel.

(a) THE ELIMINATION OF THE FORMER RESTRICTIONS AND DISTINCTIONS (56:1-8). This section opens with Yahweh's statement that the great redemption was soon to come. In order that it might not be delayed, the people were admonished to maintain the loftiest of ideals. They were to conform to the law of Yahweh, practice those virtues required in righteousness (56:1), observe the Sabbath, and abstain from evil (56:2). Those who conducted themselves according to these precepts were to be considered fortunate, for they are called "blessed." The observance of the Sabbath was divinely ordained (Genesis 2:1-3) and required in the Ten Commandments (Exodus 20:8-11); therefore, faithful sabbath observance was to be an important part of the life of the covenant people. The righteous will be known by their observance of the Sabbath and their abstention from evil.

Verses 3-8 extended the promise of salvation to the foreigner and the eunuch. This statement may have been prompted by the intolerance which existed at that time. Or perhaps this attitude on the part of the people was merely anticipated. In either case, they were to be received and can rest assured that they will never be separated from Yahweh's people (56:3). Eunuchs had been excluded from the assembly of Yahweh in accordance with the law found in Deuteronomy 23:1 which was based upon respect for the body of a person created by Yahweh. Thus, those having mutilated bodies were not considered full citizens of Israel. These eunuchs, who would never become heads of households (56:3b), were promised that they would be full members of the Israel of Yahweh. Previously, the basis of acceptance was a perfect body. But now acceptance would be based upon their faithfulness in keeping the Sabbath, their doing those things pleasing to Yahweh, and their devoted obedience to the covenant (56:4). And a special memorial would be provided for them. Since they could never expect to be memorialized in their offspring, they were to have their names memorialized on some type of monument placed in the Temple. Such a memorial was to be more highly esteemed by the entire community and more lasting ("better") than sons and daughters (56:5).

The foreigners will join with the people of Yahweh and "minister unto him, and . . . love the name of Jehovah, . . . be his servants, . . . [keep] the sabbath . . . and [hold] fast [the] covenant." They will participate in the worship, praise and prayer as though they were His very own people (56:6-8).

(b) THE TRAGIC EFFECT OF INCOMPETENT LEADERS (56:9— 57:2). After providing the foreigner and eunuch with assurance the prophet turned to those who had failed to provide proper leadership. Yahweh's watchmen (the spiritual leadership of the community) had closed their eyes to the evil which surrounded them; rather than speaking out against it, they remained "dumb" (56:10). These leaders were compared to the sheep dog that should have sounded the alarm in times of danger but had failed to do so. They were unobservant and indifferent to the peril of others, but they were intensely interested in the selfish gains to be derived from such practices as the unlawful sale of oracles (56:11). For them, the greatest thing in life was filling the day with strong drink and planning how they would pass the next one in the same drinking manner (56:12). What a tragic picture! The nation had failed; the leaders had led the populace astray. These people had seen the righteous perishing without considering the possibility of impending doom for all who were living in unrighteousness (57:1). In the midst of all this evil the righteous found peace and rest only in the grave (57:2).

(c) THE CONDEMNATION OF THE IDOLATERS (57:3-13). The prophet then turned his attention upon an unidentified group which he charged with idolatry. They may have been the wicked rulers discussed in the preceding paragraph. Some suggest that they were members of the Samaritan community. In any event, the burden of the passage was the warning that the restored community might become like her idolatrous neighbors.

The idolaters were called together so that they might hear a pronouncement of doom, and they were described in terms which indicated their idolatrous degeneracy (57:3, 4). They inflamed themselves through the most sensual practices. Their children were taken to remote places and sacrificed either to Yahweh or false gods (57:5). In these secluded spots they set up boulders which they considered sacred, and their hope was in these stones rather than in Yahweh (57:5). But Yahweh was not appeased by such practices, nor will He let them go unpunished (57:6).

Along with their idolatrous practices in the valleys, they made sacrifices to strange gods upon the mountains and hills (57:7) and worshiped household gods which were often placed behind the door or on the doorpost (57:8). The prophet, in alluding to their beds, employed the imagery of adultery — but here he was referring to spiritual adultery, idolatry.

In concluding the list of idolatries the prophet pointed to the pilgrimages made to pagan deities, including the gods of the underworld, Sheol (57:9). They followed after these deities even though it was demanding and vain (57:10). It profited them nothing and cost them everything.

(d) THE JUDGMENT THAT WILL COME UPON THE IDOLATERS (57:11-13). Verse 11 contains two profound questions for those who heard the prophet. The first, "Who are these nonentities whom you fear so much that you lie (present a false picture) and have not remembered me, nor considered the consequences of your acts?" The second, "Have not I held my peace for a long time, and you do not fear me?" Here the prophet was suggesting that they were interpreting the silence of Yahweh as a reason to fear Him no longer. When the idolaters came under His judgment, their gods would not be able to deliver a single one of them. The gods themselves will be unable to survive the judgment, for they are of so little consequence that the wind will topple them and a breath will bear them away (57:13a) On the other hand, those who took refuge in Yahweh will one day possess the Promised Land, including its Holy City (57:13b).

(e) THE BLESSINGS PROMISED THE HUMBLE AND CONTRITE (57:14-21). This section refers to the promise of verse 13 as many suggest. It does, indeed, elaborate upon it. At the outset, the instruction to "cast ye up" was a reference to the highway which would be constructed for the return of the true followers of Yahweh (57:14a). Every impediment will be removed (57:14b); nothing will be allowed to stand in the way. In contrasting Yahweh with the idols, the prophet characterized Him as "high and lifted up" and as the One dwelling in eternity whose name was Holy. Nevertheless, He was the One who dwelt with those of a contrite and humble spirit, for they had sustained life's sorrows and hurts and had rested in the quiet confidence of His presence and power (57:15).

Yahweh had punished His people in the past, but He will not afflict them beyond the point of endurance (57:16). It was necessary that Israel be disciplined because of her covetousness and backsliding (57:17). But even so, Yahweh had looked upon the nation's unhappy condition with compassionate eyes and was planning in due time to heal and restore her (57:18). Those in Jerusalem, as well as those in the exile, will be granted the peace for which they have so long yearned (57:19).

Not so for the wicked! Their lives will be as the waters of the tempesting sea, which in their tortured restlessness continue to stir up "mire" and "dirt" and never experience a period of rest and quiet. "There is no peace . . . to the wicked" (57:21).

(f) THE MERIT OF TRUE RELIGION (58:1-14). Because of the nation's persistent practices the prophet was summoned to reveal the futility of the religious observances with their perfunctory formalities (58:1). The people did not lack zealousness — that was not their trouble — they were most diligent, even eager. But they believed this was the way to establish a proper relationship between Yahweh and the nation (58:2), and it was this attitude which was their real problem. Neither their diligence nor their eagerness produced the desired results (58:3a). They failed because salvation rests not upon formal religious practice but upon righteousness (58: 3b-5).

Yahweh was not concerned with fasting which was performed in a thoughtless or selfish manner, and which was engaged in only for public show. The type of fasting pleasing to Him would have tangible results: oppressive acts ceasing and being replaced by deeds of kindness and benevolence (58:6, 7). When such deeds become a reality in their lives, a new day will dawn for them and Yahweh will immediately respond to their every need and petition (58:8, 9a).

Verses 9b-12 set forth conditions for acceptance by Yahweh similar to those found in verses 6, 7. Following this reiteration, the prophet called the people's attention once more to the potentials in the proper observance of the Sabbath (58:13, 14; cf. Isaiah 56: 2). To observe the Sabbath properly, it was necessary for them to abstain from their own pleasure and give themselves heartily to the purposes and possibilities of the day (58:13). Then, and only then, will Israel be exalted and receive the benefits of those promises which Yahweh so long ago had made to Jacob (58:14).

(g) THE LENGTHENED HAND AND THE LIGHTENED EAR (59: 1-21). Chapter 59 is a continuation of the discourse in chapter 58. Verses 1 and 2 disclose the reason Yahweh's promises had not been fulfilled. It was not because Yahweh's hand had been shortened nor because His ear could not hear the people's pleas for deliverance (59:1). They had not been ushered into the new age because their evil deeds had fixed a gulf between Yahweh and the nation (59:2): The misdeeds which had created this gulf were then stated. Their hands were covered with the blood of the innocent and their tongues muttered lies and wickedness (59:3). Lawsuits were conducted in the courts with no regard for righteousness or truth (59:4). They brooded over schemes and brought forth projects which were deadly to others and of no profit to themselves (59:5, 6). Then, as though by way of summary, the prophet pointed out that they would never know peace and justice so long as they delighted in their evil ways (59:7, 8).

Yahweh demanded righteousness, but because of the injustices in the land there was no righteousness. Since the people could not be delivered by Him so long as these injustices continued, they re-

mained in darkness rather than dwelling in the light of the new age
(59:9). They groped along in helplessness hoping to find a way
of escape, but they could find no relief. Even at noonday, when
they might have expected to find relief, there was none (59:10).
Therefore, they gave vent to their anguish by roaring like bears
and moaning like doves (59:11). It has been suggested that the
extremes of violent and gentle grief are represented in the analogy of
the bear and the dove, and this may well be the case.

The prophet, speaking in behalf of the people, confessed the
sins with which they had been charged (59:12-15a); and it was
quite an impressive list of wrongs which engulfed their society.
Wrong was so prevalent that an individual could not turn from it
without becoming the victim of those who insisted upon continuing
in it. Yet, despite all the hopelessness and desperation brought about
by the prevailing conditions, in the end Yahweh will make possible
the anticipated salvation (59:15b-17).

Yahweh saw the condition of the community and it displeased
Him that Israel had not been vindicated (59:15b). The people of
Israel were without a champion, so He committed Himself to become their champion in order that He might bring salvation to them
(59:16). Isaiah used the picture of a warrior to show God putting
on the zeal for right as a coat of mail, the helmet as salvation, a
mantle of fury in vengeance (59:17). After arraying Himself in
His attributes, He will mete out just recompense upon His enemies
(59:18). In turn, from one side of the earth to the other His
enemies will fear Him (59:19). In the case of Israel, however,
Yahweh will come, not as Judge, but as Redeemer (59:20; cf. Romans 11:26). When Israel had been redeemed, and the Spirit of
Yahweh had come upon her, she was to exert a continued spiritual
influence by means of the words He put in her mouth (59:21).
Through the abiding presence of His Spirit and the continuing possession of His Word — the basis of Yahweh's covenant with Israel
— there will be established an everlasting relationship (cf. Jeremiah
31:31-34).

2. *The Everlasting Glory of the New Jerusalem* (60:1-22).
Zion, pictured as a prostrate woman in a dark world, was commanded to "arise" and shine forth with the light and glory of
Yahweh's presence (60:1, 2). Then, upon seeing the light, the
nations of the earth will come to Zion that they might behold her
salvation (60:3).

The prophet called upon those remaining in Zion to lift up their eyes and witness the approach of those who had been in exile (60:4). When the exiles returned they were to be followed by the wealth of the nations, borne across the seas and deserts of the East as gifts to Yahweh; and as a result of this inpouring of riches His house will be gloriously beautiful (60:5-7). Verses 8 and 9 tell about the ships from the West bringing the resources of the nations to Zion.

Through Jehovah's favor, and with the resources of the nations, the city of Zion will be rebuilt in splendor (60:10-14). The wealth brought to the city will be so great that her gates will have to stand open in order that it all might be deposited within her walls (60:11). And those nations that had formerly oppressed Zion will come to pay homage to her out of respect for the light which will shine forth from the New Jerusalem (60:14).

Verses 15 and 16 describe the contrast between the attitude which the nations formerly had toward Zion and that which will be expressed toward her in the future.

The last part of the chapter pictures the land at peace through the glory of Yahweh's presence. Violence will be gone forever; the walls and gates of the city will insure safety for the occupants and evoke praise from those entering (60:18). There will be no need for light either by day or by night, because the light of His presence would supersede all other illumination (60:19). This light will not rise and set as do the luminaries, but will be an everlasting radiance which dispels darkness and drives away all mourning and unrighteousness (60:20, 21). In that day, those who had been least in the nation will be first in the purposes of Yahweh (60:22).

3. *The Purpose and the Effect of the Servant's Mission* (61:1-11). There is no general agreement among Old Testament scholars as to the identity of the speaker in this passage. There are those who contend that the "anointed one" refers to the prophet, although such a reference to himself this way is most unusual. A prophet might have been characterized as being empowered by the Spirit, but it is to be questioned that he was described as anointed. On the other hand, there seems to be every reason for identifying the "anointed one" as the Servant. In this case, as in the other Servant passages, some maintain that the Servant is Israel. But in these comments, this section will be interpreted as referring to the purpose

and effect of the Messiah's mission, as were previous passages of this nature.

(a) THE PURPOSE OF THE SERVANT'S MISSION (61:1-3). The Servant, empowered by the Spirit of Yahweh, was appointed to bring the good news of salvation to the afflicted, proclaim liberty to the captives, announce the day of Yahweh's favor and comfort the mourners of Zion (61:1-3). Those who had been so long with the ashes of mourning upon their heads will now wear turbans, a head-piece of dignity, and they will find mourning replaced with joy and honor comparable to that which marked the life of one who had been anointed (cf. Psalm 23:5). The failing spirit ("spirit of heaviness") will give way to one of buoyant praise glorifying Yahweh.

(b) THE EFFECTS OF THE SERVANT'S MISSION (61:4-11). As a result of the work of the Servant the ancient ruins will be rebuilt (cf. 49:8, 58:12, 60:10), and the foreigners who had so long enslaved Israel would become her servants (61:4, 5). Israel will be a nation of priests and ministers in a world which does not have the privations of the past. Even the glory which the nations had known will become the glory of Israel (61:6) — the full extent of the promise is shown more clearly when the last clause of the verse is translated "to their glory shall ye succeed."

Through the mission of the Servant, Israel will be repaid two-fold for the shame and dishonor she had suffered at the hands of her oppressors (61:7). Yahweh will make an everlasting covenant with her; she will never again suffer the afflictions of the past and He will never again withdraw His mercy (61:8, 9).

In verses 10 and 11, the nation, or perhaps Zion, responds to the promises of the covenant. There will be great rejoicing and joy in the goodness of Yahweh. There will also be unbounded assurance, for as certain as seed sprouts from the soil, so will Yahweh accomplish His word.

4. *The Determination of the Servant to Succeed* (62:1—63:6). Yahweh had purposed the redemption of Zion, and she was encouraged by His assurance of restoration (62:1); the world will be made to see her righteousness and recognize her relationship to Yahweh (62:2, 3). She will no longer be forsaken nor desolate and will be called 'Hephzi-bah ("my delight is in her"). She will be the wife of Yahweh and He will rejoice over her in their new relationship (62:4, 5).

Verses 6-9 contain assurances that Yahweh will not forget His promises to Zion. Watchmen had been stationed upon the walls of Jerusalem so that Yahweh will be reminded of His pledges to her (62:6-7). Some have regarded these watchmen as symbols, but in all likelihood they were prophets. He had determined that never again will others profit from the fruits of Israel's labor. To Israel herself will belong these first fruits, and they will be eaten with joy in the presence of Yahweh (62:8, 9; cf. Deuteronomy 12:17 ff., 14:23 ff.).

The last paragraph in this chapter (62:10-12) contains directions to be followed in making ready for the return of the exiles to Zion. Zion herself is instructed to prepare for their salvation (62:10, 11), for she will then be recognized as "The holy people, The redeemed of Jehovah . . . be called Sought out, A city not forsaken" (62:12).

Although Israel will know the favor of Yahweh, the nations will feel His vengeance (63:1-6). This passage pictures the aftermath of His judgment upon Israel's enemies. The Divine Hero, marching forth from Edom clothed in garments stained with the blood of the enemies of His people and the opponents of His purpose, appears as One who has been trampling the wine press.

Since there is no known historical event which corresponds with the incidents recorded in this passage, it is most frequently categorized as apocalyptic. Here, Edom stands as a representative of all the enemies of Yahweh. But none will escape; they will all be overthrown in the end.

5. *The Prayer of Israel For Mercy and Help* (63:7—64:12). Following the horrible picture of Yahweh's destruction of the nations, there is a moving prayer by the prophet. It begins with thanksgiving for Yahweh's past goodnesses in the days of Israel's youth, when "He bare them and carried them" through the wilderness on their way to the Promised Land (63:7-9).

That happy relationship did not last because Israel rebelled against Yahweh (63:10). Thus, He found it necessary to turn upon His chosen ones, and it grieved Him greatly. Yet, when His enmity was expressed toward Israel, she remembered His grace which she had experienced in the Exodus from Egypt (63:11-14). With the sure-footedness of horses or cattle in their natural habitat, Yahweh had led Israel through the sea to her resting place in Canaan.

By reason of these past favors, the prophet turned to petition and pleaded with Yahweh to remember that He was their "Father" and "Redeemer from everlasting" (63:16). They were then so few that neither Abraham nor Jacob (Israel) would be able to recognize them as their descendants (63:16). Then the prophet called upon Yahweh to deliver the people from their guilt and its tragic consequences (63:17-19). After the entreaty to remember Israel and deliver her, there followed an appeal for an overwhelming demonstration of His power (64:1-3). Only Yahweh worked wonders for those who waited in righteousness; there was no other who would do so (64:4).

In verse 5 is found the heart of the entreaty, which was based upon the confession that they have sinned. The people had long been in their sins, but none had turned to Yahweh because sin had blotted out His face from them (64:8-12). Isaiah appealed to Him as Father — they were His own creation; He had made them. Therefore, Yahweh was entreated to put away their sins and, by reason of their tragic condition, to rescue and restore them (64:9-12).

6. *The New Heavens and the New Earth* (65:1—66:24). After the prophet's heart-rending entreaty for mercy and help, Yahweh's response to the prayer is given.

(a) YAHWEH'S RESPONSE TO THE PRAYER (65:1-16). Yahweh declared that He had always stood ready to respond to them, but that the people had scorned His invitation (65:1, 2). They had provoked Him to wrath by their shameful practices (65:3-5), and in His wrath He had pronounced His judgment upon them (65:6, 7). Since Israel was precious to Yahweh, that alone promised a bright future (65:8-10). Nevertheless, those who persisted in their evil ways must be destroyed (65:11, 12).

Verses 13-16 contrast the future condition of those who had forsaken Yahweh with that which might be expected by those who in faith had submitted to Him. The faithful will find that the previous conditions had passed away, and the glories of the new universe and the new age will make them forget all that had been in the past (65:16).

(b) THE GLORIES OF THE NEW HEAVEN AND EARTH (65:17-25). In the age to come, a whole new universe will minister to the needs of Yahweh's people. The concept of a new creation has appeared before (11:6-9, 30:23 ff.), but not as clearly delineated as here. Perhaps the idea was that the present universe will *pass away* (see 51:6). Yet some have questioned whether this was no more than an expression of the impermanence of the material in contrast with the abiding nature of the spiritual. Be that as it may, this passage must be taken literally. The people of Yahweh were assured of long happy lives and abiding security (65:18-20). Jerusalem will be filled with joyful occupants who live out their days in happiness and peace. Although the prophet had not grasped the full concept of eternal life, he anticipated a limitation to death, and this was a step in the development of the theology of eternal life. He also anticipated the day in which the nations will no longer deprive Yahweh's people of the fruits of their labor (65:21-23). It will be a day of peace, when Yahweh will respond to their needs before they prayed or during their prayers (65:24). Even the serpents will cease to be harmful, for there will be no hurt in all the new creation (65:25).

(c) EVENTS LEADING UP TO THE NEW AGE (66:1-24). The new era will consist of more than the rebuilding of a house for Yahweh. In fact, the people will not be able to build one large enough to contain the presence of the One whose throne is heaven and whose footstool is the earth (66:1). But Yahweh will be less interested in the kind of house they build than the kind of spirit they possess (66:2). Without the proper spirit all else will be abominable to Him (66:3). In the past these people had not responded to His call, nor had they sacrificed that in which He found delight (66:4). Verses 5 and 6 contain assurances that they will see the wrath of Yahweh fall upon their oppressors.

Zion will bring forth a new people before the pangs of childbirth were felt (66:7). Such an occurrence was unbelievable; nevertheless, it will come to pass. Nothing can prevent Yahweh's accomplishing His purpose — the repopulation of Zion with exiles (66: 8, 9). In light of these promises for the future, the faithful remaining in Zion were told to rejoice in the prospects for Zion and her children (66:10, 11). She will again know comfort and plenty (66:13, 14). All these things will be accomplished at the time of Yahweh's judgment upon the wicked (66:15-17).

Verses 18-22 describe the conditions which will exist after the restoration of the exiles. The nations of the world will make their way to Zion to behold the glory of Yahweh (66:18). There they will witness a miracle ("sign"), and it will so impress the survivors of the judgment that they will pass through their lands declaring His glory (66:19). Then the nations will bring back the captives of Yahweh's people as if they were an offering to Him (66:20, 21).

The final paragraph of Isaiah contains a word of assurance concerning the permanent and abiding nature of the new community of Yahweh (66:22). Month by month, and Sabbath by Sabbath, mankind will go up to Jerusalem to worship before Him (66:23). But the worshipers will go forth from worship, perhaps to the Valley of Hinnom, and there they will see the dead, those who had rebelled against Yahweh (66:24).

Thus the book of Isaiah closed with a note of solemnity, a warning for the people of ancient Israel. God had sovereignty over all of history, and He punished sin whenever and wherever He found it. God still has sovereignty over all nations, and history is still working to accomplish His purpose. The times have changed, but He has not. Is it not then necessary that we, even as His people of old, take heed of this solemn warning? Should not we, too, turn to God, lest we also come under His judgment? "If ye be willing and obedient, ye shall eat the good of the land: but if ye refuse and rebel, ye shall be devoured with the sword; for the mouth of Jehovah hath spoken it" (1:19, 20).

## FOR FURTHER STUDY OR DISCUSSION

1. Do men establish superficial differences between the righteous and unrighteous? What are some of them? Does a proper relationship with God eliminate these? What New Testament concept is involved here?

2. Are leaders still responsible for conditions in the nations? How do you relate this to individual freedom?

3. Have the humble and contrite always seemed to have a place in Yahweh's purpose? What do these qualities suggest?

4. Can one be sincere in his religious practice and be wrong? What does salvation rest upon?

5. Does a delay in the judgment of God suggest for many no judgment at all? If so, why? What does it suggest for you?

6. Is there a way for the nations to be secure without military might? How? Will such a time ever come? Under what conditions?

7. What conditions are suggested for "the New Heaven and Earth"?

# ORDER
# BIBLE STUDY COMMENTARIES
## The Ideal Commentary for Study Groups

### Old Testament
- [ ] Genesis (Wood)          34743-2
- [ ] Exodus (Huey)          36053-6
- [ ] Leviticus (Goldberg)          41813-5
- [ ] Joshua (Enns)          44041-6
- [ ] Job (Garland)          24863-9
- [ ] Isaiah (Garland)          24853-1
- [ ] Jeremiah (Huey)          36063-3
- [ ] Daniel (Wood)          34723-8
- [ ] Amos (Garland)          24833-7
- [ ] Hosea (Garland)          24843-4
- [ ] Malachi (Isbell)          41673-6

### New Testament
- [ ] Matthew (Vos)          33883-2
- [ ] Mark (Vos)          33873-5
- [ ] Luke (Gideon)          24973-2
- [ ] John (Hobbs)          26113-9
- [ ] Acts (Vaughan)          33513-2
- [ ] Romans (Vaughan/Corley)          33573-6
- [ ] Galatians (Vaughan)          33543-4
- [ ] Ephesians (Vaughan)          33533-7
- [ ] Philippians (Vos)          33863-8
- [ ] Colossians and Philemon (Vaughan)          33523-X
- [ ] Thessalonians (Walvoord)          34071-3
- [ ] Pastoral Epistles, The (Blaiklock)          21233-2
- [ ] James (Vaughan)          33553-1
- [ ] I, II, III John (Vaughan)          33563-9

Visit your local bookstores or call toll free

**1-800-253-4475**

RETAIL MARKETING SERVICES
1420 Robinson Rd., S.E.
Grand Rapids, MI 49506

# NOTES

# NOTES